Mary Hickey

WARM WELCOME
cozy quilts for baby

Martingale®
& COMPANY

Warm Welcome: Cozy Quilts for Baby
© 2009 by Mary Hickey

That Patchwork Place® is an imprint of
Martingale & Company®.

Martingale & Company
19021 120th Ave. NE, Suite 102
Bothell, WA 98011-9511 USA
www.martingale-pub.com

Printed in China
14 13 12 11 10   8 7 6 5 4 3 2

Library of Congress Cataloging-in-Publication Data
Library of Congress Control Number: 2009003182

ISBN: 978-1-56477-895-6

credits

President & CEO ★ Tom Wierzbicki

Editor in Chief ★ Mary V. Green

Managing Editor ★ Tina Cook

Technical Editor ★ Laurie Baker

Copy Editor ★ Marcy Heffernan

Design Director ★ Stan Green

Production Manager ★ Regina Girard

Illustrator ★ Laurel Strand

Cover & Text Designer ★ Shelly Garrison

Photographer ★ Brent Kane

mission statement

Dedicated to providing quality products
and service to inspire creativity.

contents

preface

Babies, small and beautiful, are a force of nature. Their tiny hands take our breath away. Their petite noses and rosebud lips leave us in awe of the mystery that produces such perfect creatures. Every encounter with a baby creates in us the drive to nurture and shelter the wee one. Quilting satisfies this drive in many ways. Of course quilts provide warmth for the babies that we love. More than that, though, quiltmaking allows us to make a piece of art that expresses our dreams for our tiny friends. Making a quilt is, in a sense, a way for us to influence the future. A quilt says, "I was here and I loved you even before you were born." Quilting provides us with the opportunity to create something of lasting beauty, but much more, it can carry our message of love and tenderness into the future and influence a young life.

1

introduction

I designed the quilts in this book to be easy to make, straightforward, and uncomplicated. I made most of the quilts with simple fabrics and color combinations that make it easy for you to see the block designs. If this will be your first quilt, or if you are an experienced quiltmaker who needs to whip up a quick quilt, then "Small Checks" (page 20), "Nine-Patch Star" (page 28), "Little Dominoes" (page 44), or "Alphabet Four Patch" (page 48) are good choices because they are exceptionally quick and easy. If you have an irresistible novelty or conversation print, consider making "Apple Tree Lane" (page 40), "Picnic Patches" (page 36), or "Gift Block" (page 62), because these are also very simple quilts and good examples of uses for novelty prints.

"Cozy Kittens" (page 70) and "Baby Bows and Twinkle Toes" (page 66) are easy appliqué quilts and good choices if you like appliqué. Both quilts were made using fusible appliqué techniques, but the patterns could easily be converted for hand or machine methods. My cat, Calliope, modeled for

"Cozy Kittens" and my granddaughter, Ava, lent me her shoes for "Twinkle Toes."

The other quilts in the book all look complex but are really easy and remarkably clever. For example "Tender Hearts" (page 24) may have many pieces and triangles, but all the pieces are simple squares and rectangles—you never have to cut or sew a triangle to make the quilt. Another example is "Nine-Patch Star" (page 28), where a star appears in the quilt center without the effort of making a star. All the quilts give you the chance to play with color, light, pattern, and rhythm and to send a little message of welcoming love to a wee one.

As you sew, keep in mind that quilting is a form of recreation and an opportunity for expression. You will enjoy your quilt if it is accurately sewn, but don't let perfection become your only goal. Feel free to add your own personal touch to the quilt plans. Your personality and individual creativity, the work of your own hands, will transform your quilt into your own little masterpiece.

quilting ABCs

Quilts consist of three layers of fabrics stitched together to create a coverlet for warmth or a work of art. The top layer of the quilt is the part we enjoy making with pieced blocks or with figures appliquéd to a background. This book has instructions for making both pieced and appliquéd blocks.

The middle of a quilt is usually made of a fluffy material called batting. The back of the quilt is the third layer, and it can be very simple, made with just a single piece of plain fabric, or it can be more complex, constructed of beautiful fabrics or more piecing. The three layers have to be stitched together to keep them smooth and soft. We call this stitching "quilting," and you can do it by hand or by machine. The quilting can also be very simple or very complex, and it always adds soft shaping and sculpting to the quilt.

In this part of the book, I'll walk you through the process of making a quilt from start to finish.

fabrics

Choosing fabrics for a baby quilt is easy and fun. You only need small pieces of fabric, and you can be a little goofy with the colors if you want. Be sure to use only 100%-cotton fabrics for baby quilts and always prewash them. To choose the fabrics for a successful baby quilt, I suggest using one of these simple strategies.

Theme or conversation prints. A theme or conversation print is a fabric based on a theme or consisting of small images. Choose one fun fabric that you really want to work with. Then look at the colors in that fabric and pick a few of those for the rest of the quilt. Or choose one color in the print and use several shades of that color. For example, the theme-print fabric in "Small Checks" (page 20) features brown baby buggies printed on pink checks. I used that same shade of pink plus a darker one and a white print for the Small Checks blocks. The blocks create a nice frame around the

buggies and make a traditional-style quilt. I then used the brown for the inner border and the darker pink for the outer border.

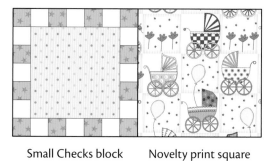

Small Checks block   Novelty print square

Nursery colors. The colors used to decorate the nursery often determine the color scheme of a baby quilt. I usually repeat the two main colors of the nursery using several shades of these colors. To keep baby quilts light and fresh, I like to use a bit of white or cream as well. "Spring Mist" (page 80) was the result of a pale green nursery; the baby of a pilot who loves red, white, and blue launched "Airplanes" (page 56); and a light beige nursery created the tone for "Cozy Kittens" (page 70).

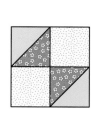 

"Spring Mist" block   "Airplanes" block

"Cozy Kittens" block

Colors you simply like. You can also choose a color scheme just because you would like to work with it. For example, "Nine-Patch Star" (page 28) is the simple combination of blue and yellow, a combination that I find brings sunshine into a quiet room. "Petite Trellis" (page 88) is just blue and lime green, a bright, contemporary color combination.

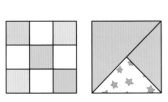 

"Nine-Patch Stars" blocks   "Petite Trellis" block

Multicolored or primary colors. When I have no real color scheme in mind and I am not using a theme print, I often make the quilt out of a variety of colors, especially two shades of the four primary colors. Bright colors are always fun to stitch.

"Little Dominoes" block

tools of the trade

There are some basic essentials you'll need for quilt-making. Buy the best equipment you can afford. Your investment in quality tools and supplies will pay off in the long run.

cutting tools

Good rotary-cutting equipment allows you to cut quickly and accurately. If you do not have rotary-cutting equipment, start by purchasing a cutter with a 45 mm blade. Check the instructions that come with it to learn the proper way to hold it and how to use the safety guard. You will also need a cutting mat on which to cut. An 18" x 24" mat is a good all-purpose size. A rotary-cutting ruler is made of 1/8"-thick acrylic and serves as a guide for the rotary cutter. The 6" x 24" size is the most essential. I also find that a 6" Bias Square® ruler is indispensable.

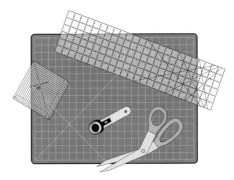

I recommend having two pairs of good-quality scissors—a large pair for cutting fabric and a small pair for cutting appliqué pieces and thread. Do not cut anything but fabric or thread with them.

sewing machine

A nice straight-stitch machine in good working order will do just about everything you need to make quilts. Take the time to get to know your machine: how it is threaded, how the functions work, and how to keep it oiled properly.

Two useful attachments for your sewing machine are a walking foot, which helps feed thick layers of a quilt through your machine more evenly when attaching bindings or machine quilting, and a darning foot for free-motion machine quilting.

Walking foot   Darning foot

needles

Replace the needle in your sewing machine regularly. An 80/12 is just right for machine piecing. I like a topstitching needle for machine quilting. For handwork, use a size 10 or 11 Sharp for hand appliqué and a size 7 or 8 Between for hand quilting.

pins

Steel straight pins with glass or plastic heads are handy for most pinning jobs. If pins are extremely thin and you sew slowly, you can leave them in place while machine sewing. Use safety pins for basting layers of the quilt together when machine quilting.

iron

Look for an iron that produces plenty of steam. Some quilters like the ones that shut themselves off if they haven't been used in a while. Other quilters like an iron that stays hot all day.

cutting your fabrics

Quiltmakers have devised a variety of clever strip-cutting and piecing techniques to use with rotary-cutting equipment. Who would ever guess that "Nine-Patch Star" (page 28) would be made from three long strips of fabric first sewn into a strip unit and then cut to make the little squares? And who could imagine that "Gift Block" (page 62) with all its little triangles could be made without ever cutting or holding a triangle in your hands? Most people think we slave away at our sewing machines for hundreds of hours when in reality we have a great time zooming along with our rotary cutters, slicing and stitching strip sets and corner triangles, and chain piecing them all together. Current quiltmaking techniques are so clever that creating a baby quilt is a genuine pleasure.

the cleanup cut

Cutting strips at an exact right angle to the folded edge of your fabric is the foundation for accuracy. Start with the first cut, known as the cleanup cut.

Fold your prewashed fabric in half with the selvages together and press. Place the fabric on your cutting mat with the folded edge closest to you. Align the fold with a horizontal line on the cutting mat. Place a 6" x 24" acrylic ruler so that the raw edges of both layers of fabric are covered and the lines of your ruler match up with the vertical grid on your mat. Hold the ruler steady with your left hand. Rolling the cutter away from you, cut along the edge of the fabric from the fold to the selvages. Remove the ruler and gently remove the waste strip. (Reverse this process if you're left-handed.)

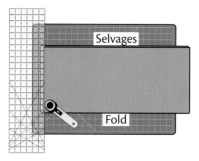

cutting strips

To cut strips, align the desired strip width on the ruler with the cut edges of the fabric. After cutting three or four strips, realign the fold of your fabric with the lines on your mat and make a new cleanup cut.

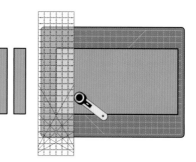

cutting squares and rectangles

To cut squares and rectangles, cut strips in the desired widths. Cut the selvage ends off the strip. Align the required measurements on the ruler with the left edge of the strip and cut a square or rectangle. Continue cutting until you have the required number of pieces. Use your ruler and periodically check that your piece measurements are accurate.

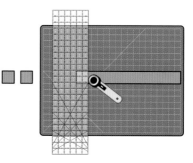

fussy cutting

We are fortunate to live in an era when thousands of adorable novelty or conversation prints are available. Two or three quilts in this book were planned specifically to enable you to use these prints successfully, and include a square in which to feature a novelty or conversation print.

Look for a quilt-block design that has a large open area where you can effectively use a little printed scene or motif. The Snowball block is my favorite. Then find another block to alternate with the Snowball block, such as the Apple Tree block in "Apple Tree Lane" (page 40).

If the motifs of the novelty print are close together and evenly spaced (which almost never happens), you can cut strips across the fabric width and then cross-cut the strips into squares. If the motifs are unevenly spaced, you will need to fussy cut the motifs. I had to do this to cut squares for "Gift Block" (page 62), "Picnic Patches" (page 36), and "Small Checks" (page 20). The border fabric for "Alphabet Four Patch" (page 48) also required some fussy cutting.

A 6"- or 12"-square ruler is useful for fussy cutting. If you are cutting many squares, place masking tape on the ruler along the appropriate markings.

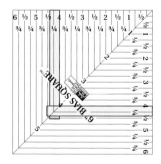

Move the marked ruler around the fabric to isolate a motif. Cut the first two sides. Next, turn the ruler around and align the desired markings with the just-cut edges. Cut the remaining two sides. If you have a limited amount of fabric, you might want to plan all your cuts first by using a pencil or a water-soluble pen to mark the cutting lines.

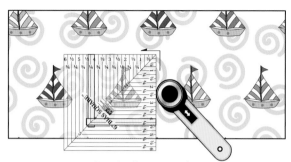

Cut the first two sides.

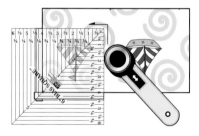

Cut the remaining two sides.

piecing your baby quilt

Now for the fun part—sitting down to sew. Make sure you have a comfortable chair and a good light.

stitch length

Set the stitch-length dial on your sewing machine to about 12 stitches per inch. When blocks are sewn directly to other blocks without sashing, the seams often need to be pinned or basted. For machine basting, set the stitch length at 6 stitches per inch. Stitch the blocks together. Check to be sure the seams match nicely. If they don't match, the 6 stitches per inch allows you to easily pick out the seams and try again. When the seams match nicely, stitch with the standard 12 stitches per inch.

the ¼" seam allowance

All of the measurements for the quilts in this book are based on using an exact ¼" seam allowance. You might be able to purchase a special ¼" presser foot for your machine. You can use the edge of the presser foot to guide the edge of the fabric for a perfect ¼" seam allowance. If you do not have a ¼" foot for your machine, take a few minutes to establish an exact ¼" seam guide on your machine.

1. Place your ruler or a piece of graph paper with four squares to the inch under the presser foot. Slide it around until you have the needle right above the ¼" line on the right-hand side of the ruler or paper. Gently lower the needle until it sits precisely on that ¼" line.

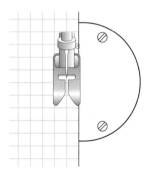

2. Make a thick guide by layering five strips of masking tape on your cutting mat (one piece right on top of the other).

3. Look at the area to the right of the ruler or graph paper, which is still under your needle and presser foot. If the feed dogs of your machine extend out to the right of the presser foot, use a pencil to draw a notch on the masking tape guide. Draw the notch about the same size as the exposed feed dogs. Use paper scissors to cut away the notched area.

4. Using the ruler or graph paper as a guide, lay the masking tape on the deck of the sewing machine so that the side of the tape with the notched edge butts up to the right edge of the ruler or graph paper. Guide your fabric along the edges of the tape. Because the tape is very thick, you will find it easy to keep the fabric on track.

chain piecing

After perfecting the ¼" seam allowance, organize yourself with the same eagerness as an Olympic athlete—prepare for a sewing marathon! Align the two fabrics you are stitching and place them under the presser foot. Lower the presser foot and hold the two thread ends. Continue to hold the threads while the machine sews the first few stitches.

When you have sewn the first pair of pieces or strips, leave them in the machine and feed the next pair in without cutting the first pair. This will save you much time and thread. Organize all the pieces that are to be joined right sides together. Arrange them in a stack with the side to be sewn on the right.

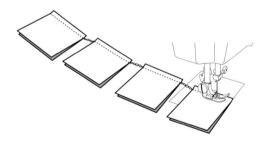

piecing-order diagrams

The instructions and illustrations for each quilt project show you the steps in which to join the pieces of your block. In general, the shortest seams will be sewn first, and you will sew progressively longer straight lines. Practice looking at quilt-block designs to see if any section can be sewn as a unit first, and then cut. If you can sew and press before cutting, you eliminate two opportunities to distort a shape after you have cut it.

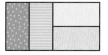

Many wonderful blocks are made up of squares. If you had to cut out 200 squares one at a time, and then sew each one to the next, the project would seem daunting. But think about cutting long strips of fabric, sewing them together, and then cutting across them to make segments or units of squares already sewn together. These are called strip sets, and they are a quick and efficient way of cutting and piecing many blocks and block units.

After sewing strips together, do a cleanup cut to remove the selvage ends of the strip set. Align the required measurement on the ruler with the cleanly cut left edge of the strip set and cut the specified number of segments. Often you will stitch the segments to other segments to make Four Patch or Nine Patch blocks.

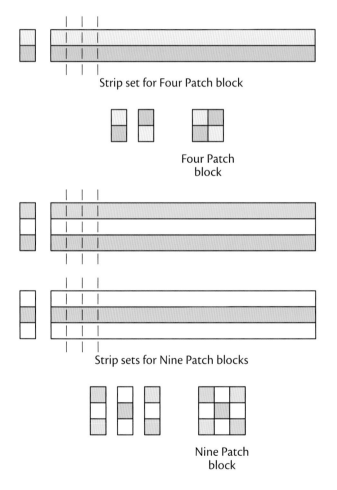

Strip set for Four Patch block

Four Patch block

Strip sets for Nine Patch blocks

Nine Patch block

half-square-triangle units

Several of the quilts in this book use half-square-triangle units (see "Spring Mist" on page 80). I make these units without cutting triangles.

"Spring Mist" block

1. Cut the square 1" larger than the desired finished size of the half-square-triangle unit. The size to cut is given in the quilt cutting instructions.

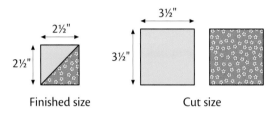

2½"

2½"

Finished size

3½"

3½"

Cut size

2. Layer the squares right sides together in pairs with the lighter color on top of the darker color.

3. Using a pencil and rotary-cutting ruler, draw a diagonal line from corner to corner on the wrong side of the lighter fabric. Sew ¼" away from the drawn line on each side. Cut on the drawn line with a rotary cutter and ruler.

4. Flip open the triangles, press the seam allowances toward the darker color, and trim away the little triangles or dog ears that extend beyond the block at the corners. Trim and square up the block to the desired unfinished size. Each pair of squares will yield two half-square-triangle units.

folded corners

One of the most satisfying tricks quiltmakers have at their disposal is a technique called folded corners. It's another way of piecing triangles without actually cutting triangles or sewing on the bias. All you do is cut squares and stitch them to the corner of another piece, usually a square or rectangle. Many of the quilts in this book feature blocks created with this technique.

1. Cut the squares the size given in the quilt instructions. Draw a diagonal line from corner to corner on the back of the squares.

2. Position the squares on the pieces called for in the quilt instructions and sew on the drawn line.

3. Cut off the corner ¼" from the seam line. Flip open the triangle and press the seam allowance toward the darker color.

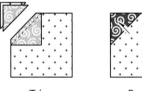

Trim.   Press.

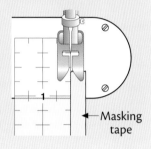
fusible appliqué

Appliqué is the process of applying fabric shapes to a larger piece of background fabric to create a design. Resourceful quilters have developed many clever methods to accomplish this time-honored quiltmaking technique. In this book, I use the fusible appliqué method.

HeatnBond, Wonder Under, and Steam-A-Seam are the brand names of some of the fusible webs available for this quick and easy fusible appliqué technique. You don't have to hem the edges of the shapes because the adhesive will prevent the edges from fraying.

1. Using a template and a pencil, draw the shapes onto the paper side of the fusible web. Note that the finished appliqué will be the reverse of the traced shape. Roughly cut out each shape about ¼" to ½" from the traced line.

Paper side of fusible web

2. Following the manufacturer's instructions, iron the shapes, fusible side down, to the wrong side of the appropriate fabrics.

3. Cut out the shapes on the traced lines.

4. Peel away the paper and position the shapes on the background fabric. Iron the shapes to the background fabric according to the manufacturer's instructions.

5. I like to topstitch the shapes with contrasting thread using a straight, zigzag, or buttonhole stitch.

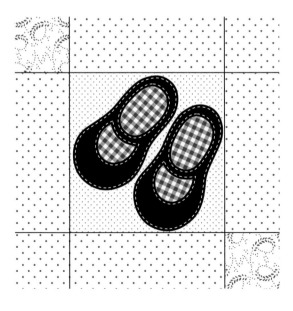

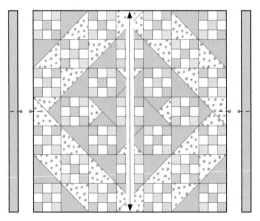
adding borders

Once you have completed your quilt top following the quilt instructions, you are ready to add borders. Borders should always be cut to fit the center measurements of the quilt. If you cut them without measuring the quilt through the center, the borders might not fit properly, and your quilts will end up looking wavy or puckered. Normal stretching during construction often leaves the edges of the quilt a little longer than the center. Sometimes each edge of a quilt is a different measurement. So measure the quilt through the center and cut the borders to fit that length. For the projects in this book, always stitch the side borders first, and then the top and bottom borders.

1. Measure the length of the quilt through the center as shown. Cut two border strips to that measurement. Mark the center of the borders and the center of the sides of the quilt top.

Measure top to bottom through the center.
Mark centers.

2. Pin, and then stitch the borders to the quilt top, matching the ends and centers and easing as necessary. Press the seam allowances toward the borders.

3. Measure the width of the quilt through the center including the side borders. Cut two strips to that measurement. Mark the center of the border strips and quilt top as you did in step 1, and then stitch the strips to the top and bottom of the quilt. Press the seam allowances toward the borders.

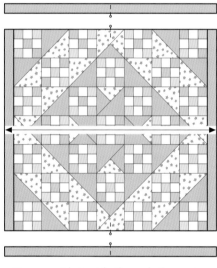

Measure side to side through the center.
Mark centers.

4. Repeat to add any additional borders.

preparing to quilt

Your quilt top is now complete and you need to decide how you will quilt it. If the design needs to be marked on the quilt, mark the design before layering the quilt with the backing and batting.

backing

Take some time when selecting the backing for your baby quilt; people will see it more than they would on an ordinary quilt. The back of most baby quilts can be made from a single piece of interesting or pretty fabric. Of course, you can also use up scraps and strips left over from the blocks to make the backing fun, funny, or pretty, depending on the quilt. You can keep it simple with a single fabric, or you can be as creative with the back of the quilt as you are with the front. Just be sure the fabric on the back does not

show through the lightest areas on the front, causing them to look dingy.

The backing should be cut 4" to 6" larger than the quilt top. If a single piece of fabric is not wide enough for the back of your baby quilt, purchase an extra half yard. Cut it in half lengthwise, stitch the two ends together, and sew it to the larger piece of backing. The following diagrams show two possible arrangements.

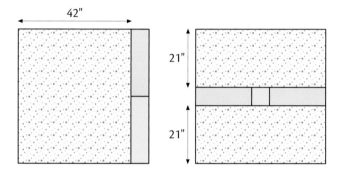

layering and basting

Press the backing fabric and quilt top. Open and unroll the batting and allow it to "relax" overnight. Spread the backing wrong side up on a clean, flat surface. Use masking tape to anchor the backing to the surface without stretching the fabric. Spread the quilt batting on the backing, making sure it covers the entire backing and is smooth. Center the pressed and marked top on the batting and backing, right side up. Align borders and straight lines of the quilt top with the edges of the backing. Pin the layers together along the edge with large straight pins to hold the layers smooth.

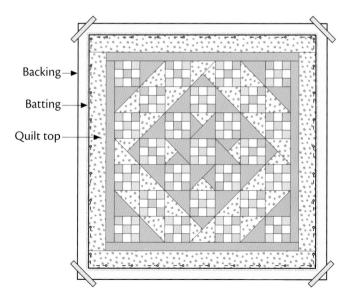

If you will be machine quilting your quilt, use 1" rustproof safety pins to baste the layers together. Start pinning in the center and work toward the outer edges of the quilt, spacing pins about 4" to 6" apart. Insert the pins as you would straight pins. Avoid pinning over design lines and seam lines where you intend to stitch in the ditch. Use a needle and thread to baste a line of stitches around the outside edges, removing the straight pins as you stitch. This will keep the edges from raveling while you quilt and also keep the edges aligned when you stitch the binding to the quilt. Remove the layered quilt from the hard surface, check the back to be sure it is smooth, and close the safety pins.

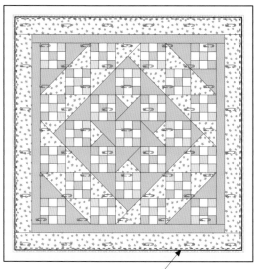

Hand baste around outer edge.

For hand quilting it is best to thread baste. Use a long needle and light-colored thread. If you thread your needle without cutting the thread off the spool, you will be able to baste at least two rows without rethreading your needle. Start at the center of the quilt and use large running stitches to baste across the quilt from side to side and top to bottom. Continue basting, creating a grid of parallel lines 6" to 8" apart. Complete the basting with a line of stitches around the outside edges. This will keep the edges from raveling while you

quilt and also keep the edges aligned when you stitch the binding to the quilt. After the basting is complete, remove all pins and masking tape.

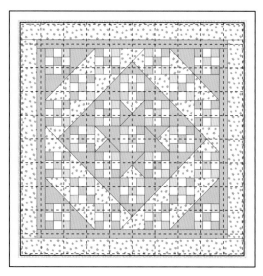

quilting

This is the time to decide whether to machine or hand quilt your baby quilt. If you have the time, hand quilting is a pleasurable and rewarding experience. Machine quilting should not be ignored, however. In the last few years it has become a beautiful art form in its own right and an excellent cottage industry for many women. Practice improves either technique.

machine quilting

Use a fine 100%-cotton silk-finish thread. Thread your bobbin with the same-quality thread. Look for a machine needle with a large eye. I like to use a top-stitching needle because it is easy to thread and will keep the thread from fraying or shredding.

walking foot

Many machines have a walking foot or even-feed foot either built into the machine or as an attachment. This moves the quilt layers through the sewing machine evenly to help prevent puckering. Use this type of foot for straight lines, grid quilting, and large, simple curves.

1. Plan a quilting design that has continuous long, straight lines and gentle curves.

2. To start and stop, shorten the stitch length for the first and last 1/8" to 1/4".

3. Roll your layered quilt up like a scroll. Starting in the center and using the walking foot, stitch all the lines from top to bottom. Always start at the same end of the quilt so that the rows won't pull in opposite directions. Re-roll your quilt from the sides and repeat stitching the straight lines in that direction. Next, repeat with the diagonal lines. Remove the pins as you secure the areas.

darning foot

When you have completed all the straight-line quilting, if you still need more quilting, switch to your darning foot, lower the feed dogs, and start the free-motion quilting. Meander quilting in the background areas gives a lovely texture and doesn't require any prior marking.

1. Pretend that you are drawing jigsaw puzzle lines or loop-de-loop curves on your quilt. Try to end up at an intersection where you can "jump" across to the next area to be stitched. To start and stop, shorten the stitch length of the first and last 1/8" to 1/4".

2. Large, open curves anchor the quilt and add softness to the quilt (see "Alphabet Four Patch" on page 48). Start at one corner and stitch in an arc to the next one.

hand quilting

Hand quilting is simply a short running stitch that goes through all three layers of the quilt. Hand quilt in a frame, in a hoop, on a tabletop, or on your lap. Use a thick thread designed for hand quilting. The thicker thread is less likely to tangle than regular sewing thread. Use a short sturdy needle (called a Between) in a size #7 or #8. Use a thimble with a rim around the top edge to help push the needle through the layers.

1. Cut the thread 24" long and tie a small knot. Starting about 1" from where you want the quilting to begin, insert the needle through the top and batting only. Bring the needle up where the quilting will start. Gently tug on the thread until the knot pops through the quilt top and catches in the batting.

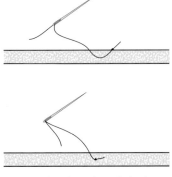

Tug on the thread until the knot goes between the layers.

2. Insert the needle and push it straight down through all the layers. Then rock the needle up and down through all layers, "loading" three or four stitches on the needle. Place your other hand under the quilt to make sure the needle has penetrated all three layers with each stitch.

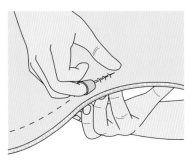

3. Pull the needle through, aiming toward yourself as you work. Continue in this way, taking small, even stitches through all three layers.

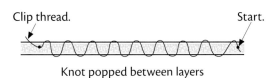

4. To end a line of quilting, make a small knot close to the quilt top, and then take one stitch through the top and batting only, bringing it up about ½" away. Pop the knot through the fabric into the batting. Clip the thread near the surface of the quilt.

Clip thread.   Start.

Knot popped between layers

finishing and binding

When all the quilting is completed, remove any stray pins and basting thread, but leave the basting stitches around the edges. Trim the batting and backing even with the quilt top. Make sure the corners are square. What a wonderful moment this is!

making a hanging sleeve

If you are going to hang your quilt, attach a sleeve or rod pocket to the back before you bind it.

1. From the leftover backing fabric cut a piece the width of your quilt by 8". On each end, fold under ½", and then fold under again; press and stitch.

2. Place the long edges wrong sides together and stitch the sleeve into a tube. Press and baste the tube to the top of the back of the quilt. When you machine stitch the binding in place you will also stitch the sleeve to the top, hiding the raw edges in the binding.

Quilt back

binding your quilt

Start by cutting binding strips. I like to make double-fold, straight-grain binding because this technique wears well and creates a smooth appearance. You can decide if you prefer to cut your strips on the lengthwise or widthwise grain of the fabric.

1. Use your rotary-cutting ruler as a guide to cut enough 2½"-wide strips to go comfortably around the quilt with about 12" extra for mitering corners and lapping the ends. Join the binding strips with diagonal seams; press the seam allowances open.

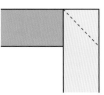

2. Fold and press the binding in half lengthwise, wrong sides together.

3. Leaving the first 10" unsewn, stitch the binding to the quilt using a ¼" seam allowance. Stop stitching ¼" from the corner of the quilt and backstitch.

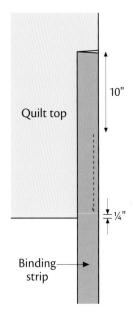

Quilt top

10"

¼"

Binding strip

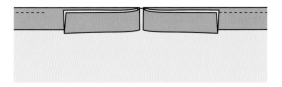

4. Remove the quilt from the sewing machine. Fold the binding away from the quilt at a 90° angle so that the fold makes a 45° angle; then fold the binding back down so it is aligned with the next side.

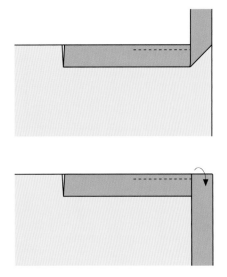

5. Using a ¼" seam allowance and beginning ¼" from the folded edge, continue stitching along the next side.

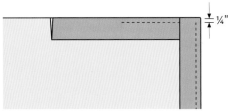

6. Continue stitching in this manner around all four sides, mitering the corners as you come to them and catching the sleeve on the top edge. Stop stitching 10" from where you started.

7. Remove the quilt from the machine and lay it on a flat surface. Fold the unsewn binding ends back on themselves so they just meet in the middle. Pin or press both strips to mark this junction.

8. Unfold both ends of the binding and mark the centers where the crease lines intersect. With right sides together, overlap the ends of the binding at right angles, matching the crease lines and marks in the middle. Pin and sew across the intersection at a 45° angle. Trim the excess fabric and press the seam allowance open.

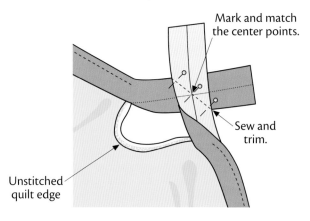

Mark and match the center points.

Sew and trim.

Unstitched quilt edge

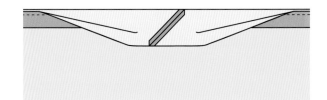

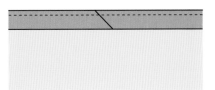

9. Finish stitching the binding to the quilt edge.

10. Fold the binding around to the back of the quilt and blindstitch it down using your machine stitching line as a guide. A miter will form at each corner. Fold the corners in place and stitch.

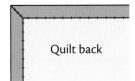

Quilt back

adding a quilt label

Labeling your quilt is an important finishing touch. A label can be as simple or as elaborate as you wish. Use a plain fabric that coordinates with your backing fabric and include the name of the quilt, your name, your city and state, date, the baby who is the recipient if it is a gift, and any other interesting or important information. This can be embroidered or written with a permanent pen. If you are using a pen, iron freezer paper to the back of the fabric before writing to stabilize the fabric. You can also make a label with your computer printer.

Nine-Patch Star
Made for Nicholas Putnam
March 24, 2007
by
"Nana"
Mary Hickey
Seattle, Washington

These delightful blocks are energetic, easy to piece, and visually stimulating with their old-fashioned buggies made from simple geometric shapes. The use of brown adds a nice contemporary touch to a traditional pink nursery. Any conversation print that you can cut into 6" to 7" squares can be used for this quilt. However, the Small Checks blocks are attractive enough that the alternate blocks can be made using just a simple print.

small CHECKS

materials

Yardages are based on 42"-wide fabric.

7/8 yard of bright pink print for Small Checks blocks and outer border

1 yard of novelty print for alternate blocks

3/8 yard of pink dotted print for Small Checks blocks

1/3 yard of white print for Small Checks blocks

1/4 yard of brown print for inner border

1/2 yard of fabric for binding

1 3/4 yards of fabric for backing

48" x 48" square of batting

cutting

From the white print, cut:
6 strips, 1 1/2" x 42"

From the bright pink print, cut:
6 strips, 1 1/2" x 42"
5 strips, 3 1/2" x 42"

From the pink dotted print, cut:
2 strips, 5 1/2" x 42"; crosscut into
   13 squares, 5 1/2" x 5 1/2"

From the novelty print, fussy cut:
12 squares, 7 1/2" x 7 1/2"

From the brown print, cut:
4 strips, 1 1/2" x 42"

From the binding fabric, cut:
5 strips, 2 1/2" x 42"

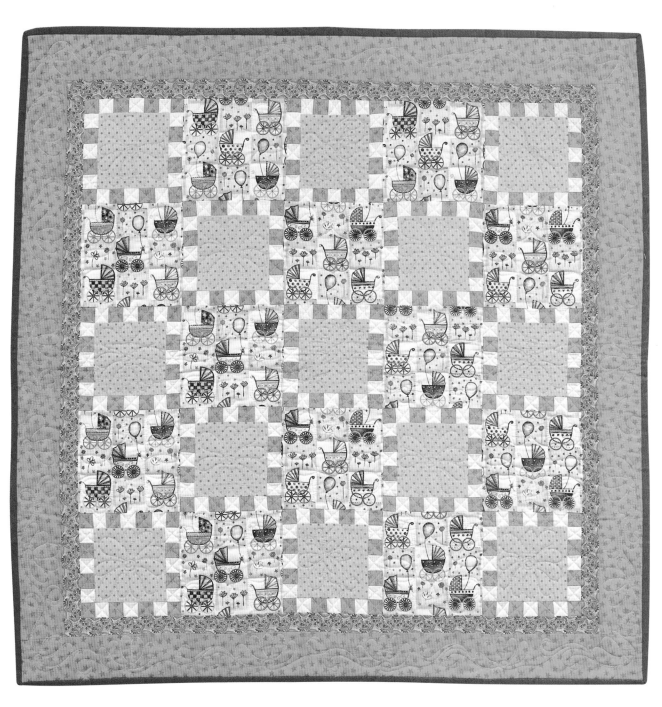

Designed and pieced by Mary Hickey. Quilted by Dawn Kelly.
Quilt size: 43" x 43" • Block size: 7" x 7"

making the small checks blocks

1. Stitch three white and two bright pink 1½" x 42" strips together as shown to make strip set A. Crosscut the strip set into 26 segments, 1½" wide.

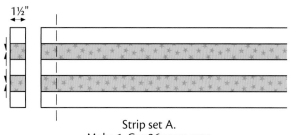

1½"

Strip set A.
Make 1. Cut 26 segments.

2. Stitch three white and four bright pink 1½" x 42" strips together as shown to make strip set B. Crosscut the strip set into 26 segments, 1½" wide.

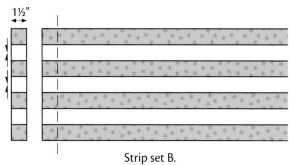

1½"

Strip set B.
Make 1. Cut 26 segments.

3. Sew a strip set A segment to the sides of each pink dotted square. Add a strip set B segment to the top and bottom of each square.

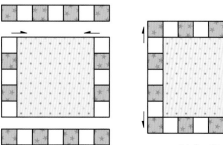

Make 13.

assembling the quilt top

1. Refer to the quilt assembly diagram to arrange the Small Checks blocks and the novelty print 7½" blocks into five rows of five blocks each, alternating the blocks in each row and from row to row. Sew the blocks in each row together, and then sew the rows together.

2. Refer to "Adding Borders" on page 13 to measure the quilt top for borders. Sew the brown 1½"-wide inner-border strips to the quilt top. Repeat with the bright pink 3½"-wide outer-border strips, piecing the strips together as necessary to achieve the required length.

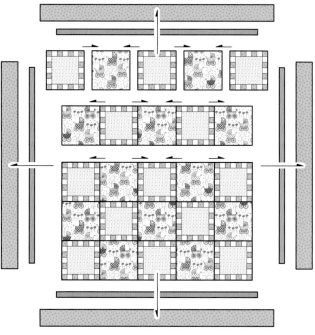

Quilt assembly

finishing the quilt

Refer to "Quilting ABCs," beginning with "Preparing to Quilt" on page 14, for more details on quilting and finishing.

1. Cut the backing fabric so it is approximately 4" to 6" larger than the quilt top.

2. Layer the backing, batting, and quilt top and baste the layers together.

3. Hand or machine quilt as desired. The quilt shown was machine quilted with lighthearted loops, flowers, and butterflies in the blocks and a floral vine in the borders.

4. Trim the batting and backing fabric so the edges are even with the quilt-top edges. Attach a hanging sleeve, if desired, and then bind the quilt. Add a label.

These adorable Heart blocks look difficult but are easily made with simple folded corners. You can see that I have arranged the light pink triangles to make a diamond shape around the little Heart blocks. This adds interest and depth to the quilt without adding difficulty.

tender HEARTS

materials

Yardages are based on 42"-wide fabric.

1⅜ yards of white print for block backgrounds and outer border

½ yard of dark pink print for hearts and inner border

½ yard of pale pink print for blocks

¼ yards *each* of 2 assorted pink prints for hearts

½ yard of fabric for binding

1½ yards of fabric for backing

43" x 43" square of batting

cutting

From the white print, cut:

3 strips, 3½" x 42"; crosscut into 24 squares, 3½" x 3½"

2 strips, 1½" x 42"; crosscut into 48 squares, 1½" x 1½"

2 strips, 1½" x 42"; crosscut into 12 rectangles, 1½" x 6½"

1 strip, 7¼" x 42"; crosscut into 1 square, 7¼" x 7¼". Trim the remainder of the strip to 7" wide and crosscut into 4 squares, 7" x 7".

1 strip, 7" x 42"; crosscut into 2 squares, 7" x 7"; cut each square once diagonally to yield 4 triangles

4 strips, 3½" x 42"

From the dark pink print, cut:

4 strips, 2" x 42"

2 strips, 3½" x 42"; crosscut into 8 rectangles, 3½" x 5½"

From *each* of the 2 assorted pink prints, cut:

2 strips, 3½" x 42"; crosscut into 8 rectangles, 3½" x 5½" (16 total)

From the pale pink print, cut:

1 strip, 7" x 42"; crosscut into 4 squares, 7" x 7"

1 square, 6½" x 6½"

1 square, 7¼" x 7¼"

From the binding fabric, cut:

5 strips, 2½" x 42"

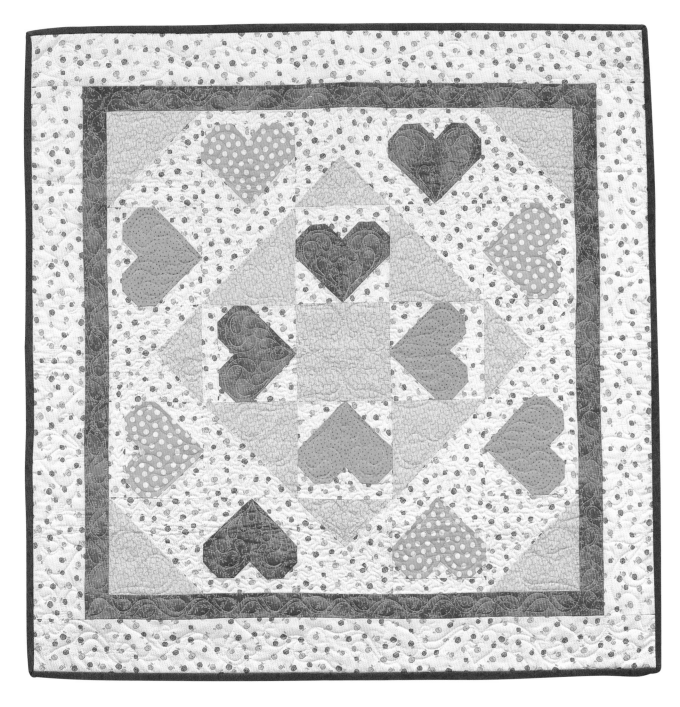

Designed and pieced by Mary Hickey. Quilted by Dawn Kelly.

Quilt size: 39" x 39" • Block size: 6" x 6"

making the heart blocks

1. Using a pencil and rotary-cutting ruler, draw a diagonal line from corner to corner on the wrong side of each white 1½" square. Refer to "Folded Corners" on page 12 to place two marked squares on each dark pink and assorted pink 3½" x 5½" rectangle as shown. Sew on the marked lines, trim ¼" from the stitching lines, flip the white triangles open, and press.

Make 24.

2. Draw a diagonal line from corner to corner on the wrong side of each white 3½" square. Select two matching rectangles from step 1. Refer to "Folded Corners" to place a marked square on each rect-angle, positioning the marked lines so they go in opposite directions on each rectangle as shown. Sew, trim, and press as before. Repeat with the remaining rectangles from step 1.

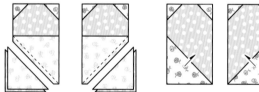

Make 12 pairs.

3. Sew the matching units from step 2 together to make a heart unit.

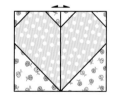

4. Sew a white 1½" x 6½" rectangle to the top of each heart unit to complete the blocks.

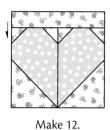

Make 12.

making the triangle blocks

1. Refer to "Half-Square-Triangle Units" on page 11 to use four white and four pale pink 7" squares to make eight Half Square Triangle blocks. Trim each block to 6½" square.

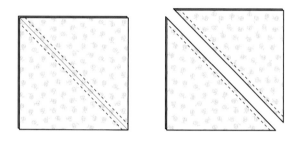

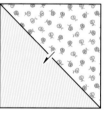

Make 8.

2. To make the Split Triangle blocks, repeat step 1 using the white and the pale pink 7¼" squares to make two half-square-triangle units, but do not trim them. Cut each unit in half diagonally to make a pieced triangle.

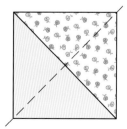

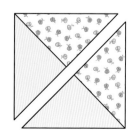

3. Sew a white triangle to each pieced triangle from step 2. Trim the blocks to 6½" square.

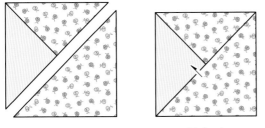

Make 4.

assembling the quilt top

1. Refer to the quilt assembly diagram to arrange the blocks and pale pink 6½" square into five rows of five blocks each. Be sure each block is oriented as shown. Sew the blocks in each row together, and then sew the rows together.

2. Refer to "Adding Borders" on page 13 to measure the quilt top for borders. Sew the dark pink 2"-wide inner-border strips to the quilt top. Repeat with the white 3½"-wide outer-border strips.

finishing the quilt

Refer to "Quilting ABCs," beginning with "Preparing to Quilt" on page 14, for more details on quilting and finishing.

1. Cut the backing fabric so it is approximately 4" to 6" larger than the quilt top.

2. Layer the backing, batting, and quilt top and baste the layers together.

3. Hand or machine quilt as desired. The quilt shown was machine quilted with echo quilting around the hearts, stippling in the white print background, vines in the inner border, and loops and hearts in the borders.

4. Trim the batting and backing fabric so the edges are even with the quilt-top edges. Attach a hanging sleeve, if desired, and then bind the quilt. Add a label.

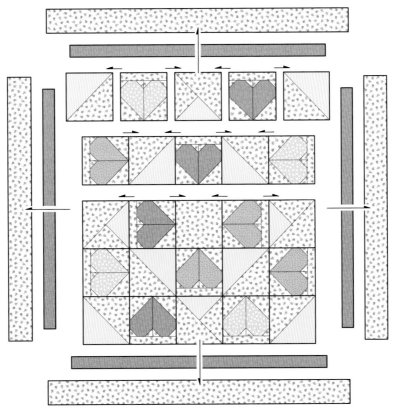

Quilt assembly

The Nine Patch block is much beloved by quilters; it's direct, straightforward, and always makes an adorable quilt. Alternating the yellow Nine Patch blocks with the blue-and-white triangle blocks creates an interesting, yet very easy quilt. You can see that by arranging the triangle blocks to create a large diamond and a star, this sparkling quilt will light up any room.

nine-patch STAR

materials

Yardages are based on 42"-wide fabric.

1 yard of white star print for triangle blocks and outer border

1 yard of blue print for triangle blocks, inner border, and binding

⅝ yard *total* of assorted yellow prints for Nine Patch blocks

½ yard of white tone-on-tone print for Nine Patch blocks

1⅓ yards of fabric for backing

45" x 45" square of batting

cutting

From the assorted yellow prints, cut a *total* of:
8 strips, 2" x 42"

From the white tone-on-tone print, cut:
7 strips, 2" x 42"

From the white star print, cut:
1 strip, 5½" x 42"; crosscut into 7 squares, 5½" x 5½"
1 strip, 6" x 42"; crosscut into 4 squares, 6" x 6". Cut 2 squares once diagonally to yield 4 triangles. From the remainder of the strip, cut 1 square, 5½" x 5½".
5 strips, 3½" x 42"

From the blue print, cut:
1 strip, 5½" x 42"; crosscut into 7 squares, 5½" x 5½"
1 strip, 6" x 42"; crosscut into 4 squares, 6" x 6". Cut 2 squares once diagonally to yield 4 triangles. From the remainder of the strip, cut 1 square, 5½" x 5½".
4 strips, 2" x 42"
5 strips, 2½" x 42"

Designed and pieced by Mary Hickey. Quilted by Dawn Kelly.

Quilt size: 40½" x 40½" • Block size: 4½" x 4½"

making the nine patch blocks

1. Sew two different assorted yellow 2" x 42" strips to opposite sides of a white tone-on-tone 2" x 42" strip to make strip set A. Repeat to make a total of three strip sets. Crosscut the strip sets into 50 segments, 2" wide.

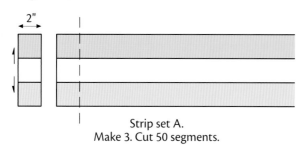

Strip set A.
Make 3. Cut 50 segments.

2. Sew two white tone-on-tone 2" x 42" strips to opposite sides of an assorted yellow 2" x 42" strip to make strip set B. Repeat to make a total of two strip sets. Crosscut the strip sets into 25 segments, 2" wide.

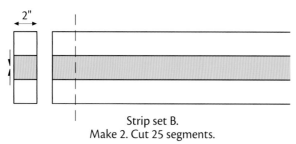

Strip set B.
Make 2. Cut 25 segments.

3. Sew together two strip set A segments and one strip set B segment as shown to make a Nine Patch block. Repeat to make a total of 25 blocks.

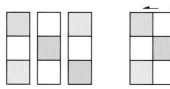

Make 25.

making the triangle blocks

1. Refer to "Half-Square-Triangle Units" on page 11 to use the white star print and blue 5½" squares to make 16 Half Square Triangle blocks. Trim each block to 5" square.

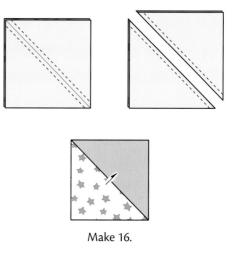

Make 16.

2. To make the Split Triangle blocks, repeat step 1 with the two white star print and two blue 6" squares to make four half-square-triangle units, but do not trim them. Cut each unit in half diagonally to make eight pieced triangles.

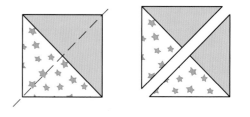

3. Sew a white star print triangle to each of four pieced triangles. Sew a blue triangle to each of the remaining four pieced triangles. Trim the blocks to 5" square.

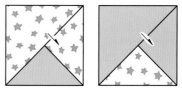

Make 4 of each.

assembling the quilt top

1. Refer to the quilt assembly diagram to arrange the blocks into seven rows of seven blocks each. Be sure each block is oriented as shown. Sew the blocks in each row together, and then sew the rows together.

2. Refer to "Adding Borders" on page 13 to measure the quilt top for borders. Sew the blue 2"-wide inner-border strips to the quilt top. Repeat with the white star print 3½"-wide outer-border strips.

finishing the quilt

Refer to "Quilting ABCs," beginning with "Preparing to Quilt" on page 14, for more details on quilting and finishing.

1. Cut the backing fabric so it is approximately 4" to 6" larger than the quilt top.

2. Layer the backing, batting, and quilt top and baste the layers together.

3. Hand or machine quilt as desired. The quilt shown was machine quilted with an X going through the Nine Patch blocks and a meandering stitch on the white print fabric.

4. Trim the batting and backing fabric so the edges are even with the quilt-top edges. Attach a hanging sleeve, if desired, and then bind the quilt. Add a label.

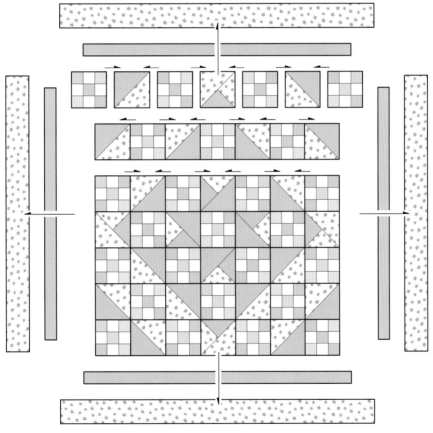

Quilt assembly

The multifaceted look of a large basket quilt is packed into this diminutive version. The quilt looks intricate and old-fashioned, but the blocks are small and quick to sew. The pastel vine print creates the color scheme of light and medium colors, which are echoed in the variety of prints used for the baskets.

nine-patch BASKETS

materials

Yardages are based on 42"-wide fabric.

1⅓ yards of vine print for setting pieces and outer border

⅝ yard of white tone-on-tone print for Basket block backgrounds

⅜ yard of medium green print for baskets and inner border

Scraps of light and medium blue prints, light and medium lavender prints, light and medium pink prints, light and medium yellow prints, and light green print for baskets

½ yard of blue print for binding

1⅝ yards of fabric for backing

43" x 52" piece of batting

cutting

From the medium green print, cut:
6 strips, 1¾" x 42"; crosscut 2 strips into:

    3 rectangles, 1¾" x 12"

    9 squares, 1¾" x 1¾"; cut 3 squares once diagonally to yield 6 triangles

From *each* of the scraps of light green and light blue, cut:
3 rectangles, 1¾" x 12" (6 total)

From the scraps of medium blue, cut:
3 rectangles, 1¾" x 12"

9 squares, 1¾" x 1¾"; cut 3 squares once diagonally to yield 6 triangles

From *each* of the scraps of light pink, light yellow, and light lavender, cut:
3 strips, 1¾" x 12" (9 total)

From *each* of the scraps of medium pink, medium yellow, and medium lavender, cut:
3 strips, 1¾" x 12" (9 total)

4 squares, 1¾" x 1¾"; cut 2 squares once diagonally to yield 4 triangles (12 total)

Designed and pieced by Mary Hickey. Quilted by Julie Goodwin.

Quilt size: 36⅝" x 45½" • Block size: 6¼" x 6¼"

From the white tone-on-tone print, cut:

7 strips, 1¾" x 42"; crosscut into:

    36 rectangles, 1¾" x 4¼"

    12 rectangles, 1¾" x 5½"

1 strip, 3⅜" x 42"; crosscut into 6 squares,
3⅜" x 3⅜". Cut each square once diagonally to
yield 12 triangles.

From the vine print, cut:

2 strips, 6¾" x 42"; crosscut into:

    6 squares, 6¾" x 6¾"

    2 squares, 5⅜" x 5⅜"; cut each square once
    diagonally to yield 4 corner setting triangles

1 strip, 10⅛" x 42"; crosscut into 3 squares,
10⅛" x 10⅛". Cut each square twice diagonally to
yield 12 side setting triangles (you will use 10).

4 strips, 4¼" x 42"

From the blue print for binding, cut:

5 strips, 2½" x 42"

making the basket blocks

1. Stitch together two medium green and one light
green 1¾" x 12" rectangles as shown to make
strip set A. Repeat with two medium and one light
blue rectangles. Crosscut each strip set into three
segments, 1¾" wide.

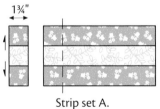

Strip set A.
Make 1. Cut 3 segments.

2. Stitch together two light and one medium green
1¾" x 12" rectangles as shown to make strip set B.
Repeat with two light and one medium blue
rectangles. Crosscut each strip set into six
segments, 1¾" wide.

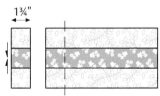

Strip set B.
Make 1. Cut 6 segments.

3. Repeat steps 1 and 2 with the medium and light
pink, medium and light lavender, and medium
and light yellow strips to make one strip set A and
one strip set B of each color family. Crosscut each
strip set A into two segments and each strip set B
into four segments, each 1¾" wide.

4. Using segments from the same color family, sew a
B segment to the sides of each A segment to make
a nine-patch unit. Make three green, three blue,
and two each of the pink, lavender, and yellow
units.

Make 3.

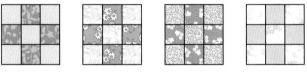

Make 3.   Make 2.   Make 2.   Make 2.

5. Using a pencil and rotary-cutting ruler, draw a
diagonal line from corner to corner on the wrong
side of each medium green, blue, pink, lavender,
and yellow 1¾" square. Refer to "Folded Corners"
on page 12 to place a marked square on one end
of 12 white tone-on-tone 1¾" x 4¼" rectangles
and 12 white tone-on-tone 1¾" x 5½" rectangles.
Sew on the marked lines, trim ¼" from the stitching lines, flip the white triangles open, and press.

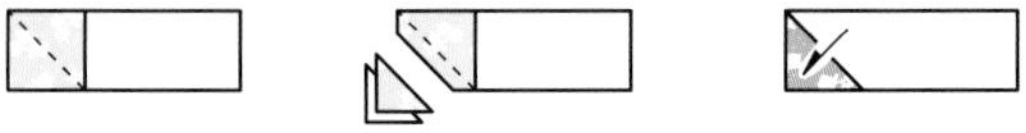

Make 3 each of
green and blue
and 2 each of pink,
lavender, and yellow.

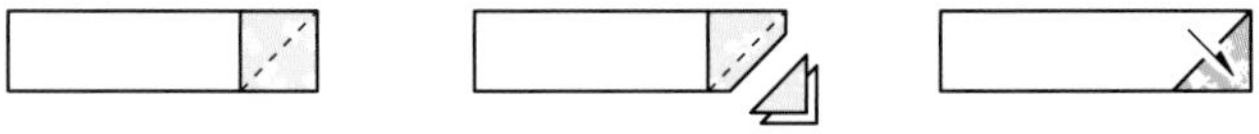

Make 3 each of
green and blue
and 2 each of pink,
lavender, and yellow.

6. Stitch the medium green, blue, pink, lavender, and yellow triangles to the ends of each of the remaining white tone-on-tone 1¾" x 4¼" rectangles as shown. Make sure each color has a triangle oriented in each direction.

Make 3 each of green and blue
and 2 each of pink, lavender, and yellow.

7. Using pieces from the same color family, stitch the units from step 5 to the top and right side of each nine-patch unit. Sew the units from step 6 to the bottom and left side of each nine patch unit. Add the white triangles to the lower edges of these units to complete the blocks. Make three green, three blue, and two each of the pink, lavender, and yellow blocks (12 total).

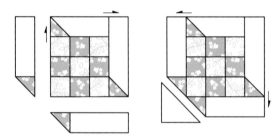

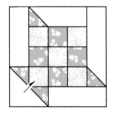

Make 12 total.

assembling the quilt top

1. Refer to the quilt assembly diagram to arrange the Basket blocks, the vine print 6¾" squares, and the vine print setting triangles into diagonal rows. Sew the pieces in each row together, and then sew the rows together, adding the corner setting triangles last.

2. Refer to "Adding Borders" on page 13 to measure the quilt top for borders. Sew the medium green 1¾"-wide inner-border strips to the quilt top. Repeat with the vine print 4¼"-wide outer-border strips.

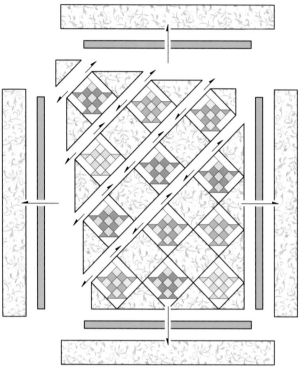

Quilt assembly

finishing the quilt

Refer to "Quilting ABCs," beginning with "Preparing to Quilt" on page 14, for more details on quilting and finishing.

1. Cut the backing fabric so it is approximately 4" to 6" larger than the quilt top.

2. Layer the backing, batting, and quilt top and baste the layers together.

3. Hand or machine quilt as desired. The quilt shown was machine quilted in the ditch in the Basket blocks, with scrollwork flowers in the plain blocks and with lighthearted vines in the borders.

4. Trim the batting and backing fabric so the edges are even with the quilt-top edges. Attach a hanging sleeve, if desired, and then bind the quilt. Add a label.

I love making this quilt as a gift because it's so simple to stitch and yet it looks like an honest-to-goodness serious quilt, cleverly giving the recipient the idea that I spent many hard hours working away on behalf of her new baby. The blocks are pretty and give that complex look we so love in a quilt. You can use a novelty print for the alternate blocks as I did or just use any simple print.

picnic PATCHES

materials

Yardages are based on 42"-wide fabric.

1 yard of novelty print for alternate blocks

²/₃ yard of muslin for pieced blocks

½ yard *total* of assorted green prints for pieced blocks

½ yard *total* of assorted pink prints for pieced blocks

½ yard of green print for outer border

¼ yard of pink print for inner border

½ yard of fabric for binding

1½ yards of fabric for backing

38" x 48" piece of batting

cutting

From the assorted pink prints, cut a *total* of:
3 strips, 1½" x 42"; crosscut *1* strip in half to make 2 half strips, 1½" x 21" (you will have 1 half strip left over)

6 sets of 4 squares each, 2" x 2" (24 total)

From the muslin, cut:
14 strips, 1½" x 42"; crosscut *3* strips in half to make 6 half strips, 1½" x 21" (you will have 1 half strip left over)

From the assorted green prints, cut a *total* of:
2 strips, 1½" x 42"; crosscut each strip in half to make 4 half strips, 1½" x 21" (you will have 1 half strip left over)

12 sets of 4 squares each, 2" x 2" (48 total)

From the novelty print, fussy cut:
17 squares, 5½" x 5½"

From the pink print for inner border, cut:
4 strips, 1½" x 42"

From the green print for outer border, cut:
4 strips, 3½" x 42"

From the fabric for binding, cut:
5 strips, 2½" x 42"

Designed and pieced by Mary Hickey. Quilted by Dawn Kelly.

Quilt size: 33" x 43" • Block size: 5" x 5"

making the pieced blocks

1. Sew two assorted pink 1½" x 42" strips to opposite sides of a muslin 1½" x 42" strip to make strip set A. Crosscut the strip set into 24 segments, 1½" wide.

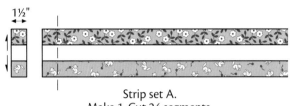

Strip set A.
Make 1. Cut 24 segments.

2. Sew two muslin 1½" x 21" half strips to opposite sides of an assorted green 1½" x 21" half strip to make strip set B. Crosscut the strip set into 12 segments, 1½" wide.

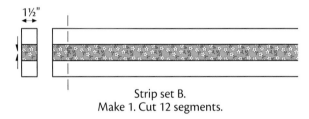

Strip set B.
Make 1. Cut 12 segments.

3. Sew A segments to opposite sides of each B segment to make 12 pink nine-patch units.

Make 12.

4. Using the green, muslin, and pink 1½" x 21" half strips, refer to steps 1 and 2 to make strip sets C and D and cut them into the number of

1½" segments shown. Refer to step 3 to sew the segments together to make six green nine-patch units.

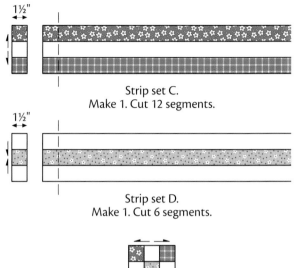

Strip set C.
Make 1. Cut 12 segments.

Strip set D.
Make 1. Cut 6 segments.

Make 6.

5. With right sides together and raw edges aligned, arrange the nine-patch units along the long edge of the muslin 1½" x 42" strips. Allow a small amount of space between each unit. Stitch along the long edge. Press the seam allowance toward the nine-patch units. Align your rotary-cutting ruler with the right edge of a nine-patch unit so that it spans the muslin strip and cut across the strip. Trim the left side of each segment even with the nine-patch unit. Repeat on the opposite side of each nine-patch unit. Make sure each unit measures 3½" x 5½".

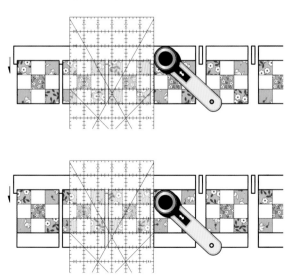

6. Repeat step 5 on the other two sides of each nine-patch unit. Make sure each unit measures 5½" x 5½".

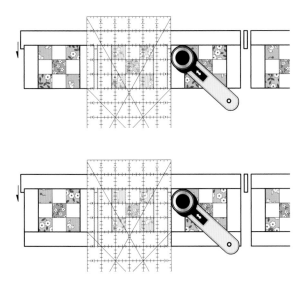

7. Using a pencil and rotary-cutting ruler, draw a diagonal line from corner to corner on the wrong side of each assorted pink and green 2" square. Using four matching green squares, refer to "Folded Corners" on page 12 to place a square on each corner of a pink nine-patch unit. Sew on the marked lines, trim ¼" from the stitching lines, flip the triangles open, and press. Repeat with the remaining nine-patch units using the green squares on the pink nine-patch units and the pink squares on the green nine-patch units.

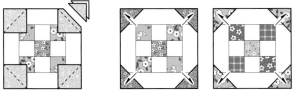

Make 12.   Make 6.

assembling the quilt top

1. Arrange the pieced blocks and the novelty print 5½" blocks into seven rows of five blocks each, alternating the blocks in each row and from row to row. Pay careful attention to the color of the pieced blocks. Sew the blocks in each row together, and then sew the rows together.

2. Refer to "Adding Borders" on page 13 to measure the quilt top for borders. Sew the pink print 1½"-wide inner-border strips to the quilt top. Repeat with the green print 3½"-wide outer-border strips.

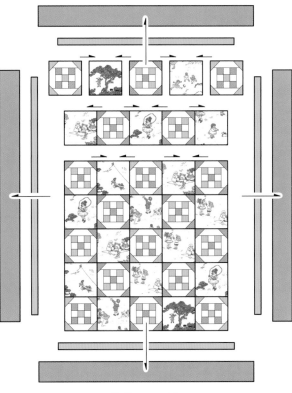

Quilt assembly

finishing the quilt

Refer to "Quilting ABCs," beginning with "Preparing to Quilt" on page 14, for more details on quilting and finishing.

1. Cut the backing fabric so it is approximately 4" to 6" larger than the quilt top.

2. Layer the backing, batting, and quilt top and baste the layers together.

3. Hand or machine quilt as desired. The quilt shown was machine quilted with a crosshatch design across the theme-print blocks, free-form curves and diamonds in the nine-patch blocks, lighthearted loops in the inner border, and curves in the outer borders.

4. Trim the batting and backing fabric so the edges are even with the quilt-top edges. Attach a hanging sleeve, if desired, and then bind the quilt. Add a label.

Simple Puss in the Corner blocks combined with Snowball blocks are a good way to use a novelty fabric in a baby quilt. Keeping a simple color palette of all greens enhances the appealing toile print. Any conversation print would be well showcased by this combination of blocks, creating a quilt that seems complex but is really quite simple and fun to make.

apple tree LANE

materials

Yardages are based on 42"-wide fabric.

1 yard of green-and-cream children's themed toile for Snowball blocks

⅝ yard of green polka-dot print for Puss in the Corner blocks and outer border

⅜ yard of pale green print for Puss in the Corner blocks and inner border

⅜ yard of green-and-cream print for Puss in the Corner blocks

¼ yard of light green print for Snowball blocks

⅜ yard of fabric for binding

1¼ yards of fabric for backing

38" x 38" square of batting

cutting

From the light green print, cut:
3 strips, 2" x 42"; crosscut into 48 squares, 2" x 2"

From the children's themed toile, fussy cut:
12 squares, 6" x 6"

From the green polka-dot print, cut:
3 strips, 2" x 42"; cut *1* strip in half crosswise to make 2 half strips, 2" x 21"

4 strips, 3½" x 42"

From the green-and-cream print, cut:
2 strips, 3" x 42"; cut *1* strip in half crosswise to make 2 half strips, 3" x 21" (you will have 1 half strip left over)

2 strips, 2" x 42"

From the pale green print, cut:
1 strip, 3" x 42"

4 strips, 2" x 42"

From the fabric for binding, cut:
4 strips, 2½" x 42"

Designed and pieced by Mary Hickey. Quilted by Julie Goodwin.

Quilt size: 34" x 34" • Block size: 5½" x 5½"

making the snowball blocks

Using a pencil and rotary-cutting ruler, draw a diagonal line from corner to corner on the wrong side of each light green 2" square. Refer to "Folded Corners" on page 12 to place a marked square on each corner of each toile square. Sew on the marked lines, trim ¼" from the stitching lines, flip the green triangles open, and press.

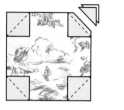 

Make 12.

making the puss in the corner blocks

1. Sew the green polka-dot 2" x 42" strips to opposite sides of the green-and-cream 3" x 42" strip to make strip set A. Repeat with the green polka-dot 2" x 21" half strips and green-and-cream 3" x 21" half strip to make a half strip set. Crosscut the strip sets into 26 segments, 2" wide.

Strip set A.
Make 1½. Cut 26 segments.

2. Sew the green-and-cream print 2" x 42" strips to opposite sides of the pale green 3" x 42" strip to make strip set B. Crosscut the strip set into 13 segments, 3" wide.

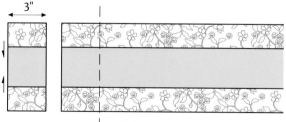

Strip set B.
Make 1. Cut 13 segments.

3. Sew A segments to opposite sides of each B segment to complete the blocks.

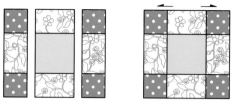

Make 13.

assembling the quilt top

1. Refer to the quilt assembly diagram to arrange the blocks into five rows of five blocks each, alternating the blocks in each row and from row to row. Stitch the blocks in each row together, and then stitch the rows together.

2. Refer to "Adding Borders" on page 13 to measure the quilt top for borders. Sew the pale green 2"-wide inner-border strips to the quilt top. Repeat with the green polka-dot 3½"-wide outer-border strips.

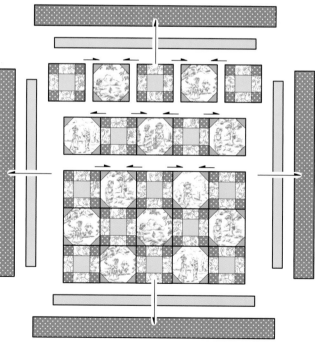

Quilt assembly

finishing the quilt

Refer to "Quilting ABCs," beginning with "Preparing to Quilt" on page 14, for more details on quilting and finishing.

1. Cut the backing fabric so it is approximately 4" to 6" larger than the quilt top.

2. Layer the backing, batting, and quilt top and baste the layers together.

3. Hand or machine quilt as desired. The toile print in the quilt shown was outline quilted, the Puss in the Corner blocks were quilted with a floral design, and the remainder of the quilt was quilted with lighthearted loops and curves.

4. Trim the batting and backing fabric so the edges are even with the quilt-top edges. Attach a hanging sleeve, if desired, and then bind the quilt. Add a label.

This quilt has fun written all over it! Pick a light background print with lots of bright colors printed on it and pair it with light and medium prints of four of the colors used. If you know the baby's gender, use the pink or blue fabrics you used in the blocks for the border, and if you don't, the green or yellow will work for either a boy or a girl.

little DOMINOES

materials

Yardages are based on 42"-wide fabric.

¾ yard of white star print for setting squares and triangles

⅝ yard of light pink-and-white print for blocks and outer border

⅜ yard of medium pink polka-dot print for blocks and inner border

¼ yard *each* of light green, medium green, light blue, medium blue, light yellow, and medium yellow prints

½ yard of fabric for binding

1½ yards of fabric for backing

40" x 48" piece of batting

cutting

From the light pink-and-white print, cut:
2 strips, 2" x 42"
4 strips, 3¾" x 42"

From the medium pink polka-dot print, cut:
2 strips, 2" x 42"
4 strips, 1½" x 42"

From *each* of the light green, medium green, light blue, medium blue, light yellow, and medium yellow prints, cut:
2 strips, 2" x 42" (12 total)

From the white star print, cut:
1 strip, 6½" x 42"; crosscut into 6 squares, 6½" x 6½"

1 strip, 9¾" x 42"; crosscut into 3 squares, 9¾" x 9¾".
   Cut each square twice diagonally to yield 12 side setting triangles (you will have 2 left over).

1 strip, 5¼" x 42"; crosscut into 2 squares, 5¼" x 5¼".
   Cut each square once diagonally to yield 4 corner setting triangles.

From the fabric for binding, cut:
5 strips, 2½" x 42"

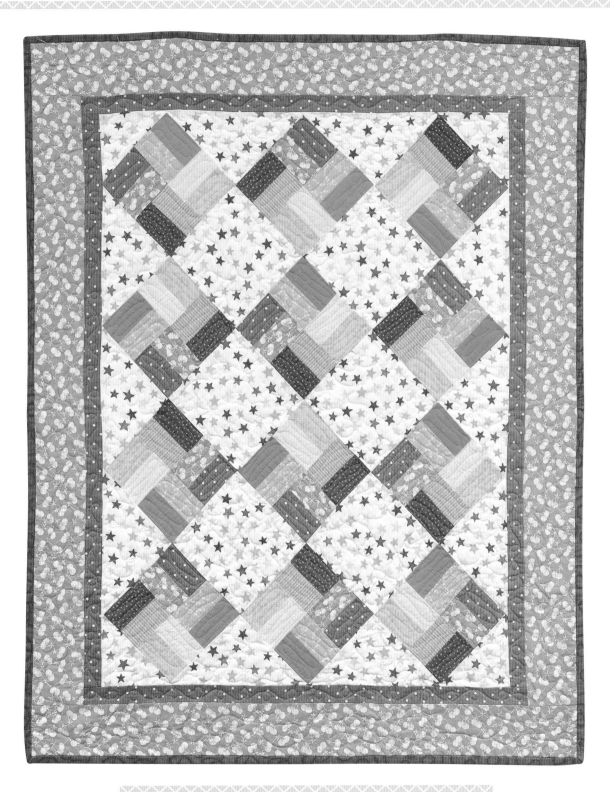

Designed and pieced by Mary Hickey. Quilted by Julie Goodwin.
Quilt size: 35" x 42½" • Block size: 6" x 6"

making the dominoes blocks

1. Stitch a light pink-and-white 2" x 42" strip to a medium pink polka-dot 2" x 42" strip to make a strip set. Repeat to make a total of two strip sets. Crosscut the strip sets into 12 segments, 3½" wide. Repeat with the light green and medium green strips, the light blue and medium blue strips, and the light yellow and medium yellow strips.

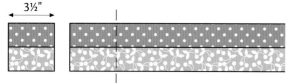

← 3½" →

Make 2 strip sets each of pink, green, blue, and yellow.
Cut 12 segments of each color.

2. Arrange one segment of each color into two horizontal rows of two segments each. The orientation of the segments does not have to be the same for each block, but the segments should alternate direction around the block. Sew the segments in each row together, and then sew the rows together. Repeat to make a total of 12 blocks.

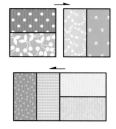 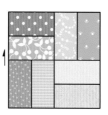

Make 12.

assembling the quilt top

1. Refer to the quilt assembly diagram to arrange the Dominoes blocks, the white star print 6½" squares, and the white star print side setting triangles into diagonal rows. Sew the pieces in each row together, and then sew the rows together, adding the corner setting triangles last.

2. Refer to "Adding Borders" on page 13 to measure the quilt top for borders. Sew the pink polka-dot 1½"-wide inner-border strips to the quilt top. Repeat with the light pink-and-white 3¾"-wide outer-border strips.

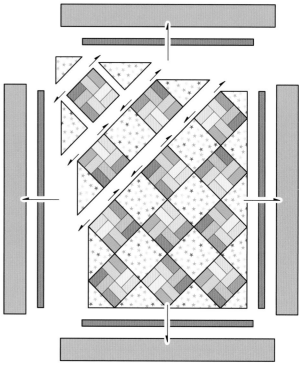

Quilt assembly

finishing the quilt

Refer to "Quilting ABCs," beginning with "Preparing to Quilt" on page 14, for more details on quilting and finishing.

1. Cut the backing fabric so it is approximately 4" to 6" larger than the quilt top.

2. Layer the backing, batting, and quilt top and baste the layers together.

3. Hand or machine quilt as desired. The quilt shown was machine quilted with lighthearted loops and stars in the white star print squares and triangles, parallel lines in the Dominoes blocks, a loopy line in the inner border, and cherries in the outer border.

4. Trim the batting and backing fabric so the edges are even with the quilt-top edges. Attach a hanging sleeve, if desired, and then bind the quilt. Add a label.

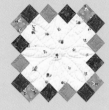

A wonderful variety of alphabet prints is available to quilters. This quilt provides an example of a nice way to use a print with letters in the border. The quilt blocks echo the colors of the letters. You can of course use an alphabet as the border for any quilt, and you can make this quilt with just a solid-colored border.

alphabet FOUR PATCH

materials

Yardages are based on 42"-wide fabric.

1 alphabet panel with light background and 2½"- to 4½"-high letters for outer border

1⅓ yards of assorted off-white prints for blocks

⅔ yard of green print for blocks and wide binding

⅜ yard of blue print for blocks and inner border

¼ yard of red print for blocks and outer-border corner squares

¼ yard of off-white fabric to match alphabet panel background for outer border

⅛ yard of yellow print for blocks and inner-border corner squares

⅛ yard of turquoise print for blocks

1⅞ yards of fabric for backing

52" x 52" square of batting

cutting

From the assorted off-white prints, cut a *total* of:
6 strips, 2" x 42"; crosscut *1* strip into 3 rectangles, 2" x 13"

5 strips, 3½" x 42"; crosscut into:
24 squares, 3½" x 3½"
12 rectangles, 3½" x 6½"

1 strip, 9¾" x 42"; crosscut into 3 squares, 9¾" x 9¾". Cut each square twice diagonally to yield 12 side setting triangles. From the remainder of the strip, cut 2 squares, 5¼" x 5¼". Cut each square once diagonally to yield 4 corner triangles.

1 square, 6½" x 6½"

Designed and pieced by Mary Hickey. Quilted by Dawn Kelly.

Quilt size: 45½" x 45½" • Block size: 6" x 6"

From the green print, cut:
1 strip, 2" x 42"
1 strip 2" x 13"
5 strips, 4" x 42"*

This width creates a wide binding. If you prefer a narrower binding, cut the strips 2½" wide.

From the blue print, cut:
3 strips, 2" x 42"
1 strip, 2" x 13"

From the red print, cut:
1 strip, 2" x 42"
1 strip, 2" x 13"

From the yellow print, cut:
1 strip, 2" x 42"; crosscut into 4 squares, 2" x 2".
    Reserve the remainder of the strip for the strip set.

From the turquoise print, cut:
1 strip, 2" x 42"

making the four patch blocks

1. Stitch an off-white 2" x 42" strip to each blue, green, red, and turquoise 2" x 42" strip and the remainder of the yellow 2"-wide strip to make strip sets. Stitch an off-white 2" x 13" strip to each blue, green, and red 2" x 13" strip to make one-third strip sets. Crosscut each strip set into the number of 2"-wide segments indicated.

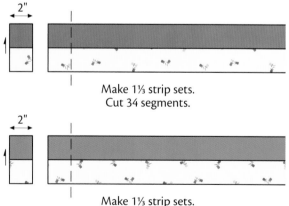

Make 1⅓ strip sets.
Cut 34 segments.

Make 1⅓ strip sets.
Cut 24 segments.

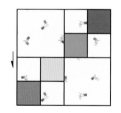

Make 1⅓ strip sets.
Cut 24 segments.

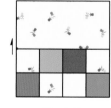

Make 1 strip set.
Cut 12 segments.

Make 1 strip set.
Cut 12 segments.

2. Stitch the segments together in pairs as shown to make four-patch units.

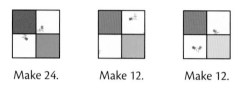

Make 24.   Make 12.   Make 12.

3. Sew the four-patch units and the off-white 3½" squares and 3½" x 6½" rectangles together as shown to make Four Patch blocks A and B.

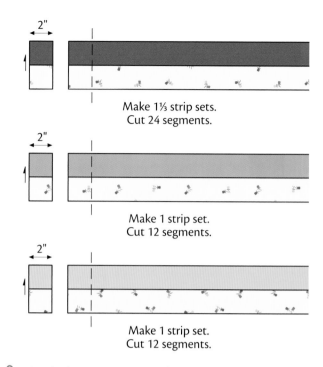

Block A.   Block B.
Make 12.   Make 12.

assembling the quilt top

1. Refer to the quilt assembly diagram to arrange the Four Patch blocks, the off-white 6½" square, the off-white side setting triangles, and the off-white corner setting triangles into diagonal rows. Sew the pieces in each row together, and then sew the rows together, adding the corner setting triangles last.

2. Measure the quilt top through the center from top to bottom and trim two of the blue 2" x 42" strips to this measurement for the side borders. Measure the quilt top through the center from side to side and cut the remaining two blue 2" x 42" strips to this measurement for the top and bottom borders. Sew the side borders to the sides of the quilt top. Add a yellow 2" square to the ends of the top and bottom border strips. Sew these strips to the top and bottom edges of the quilt top.

3. Measure the quilt top through the center from top to bottom and from side to side and make a note of each measurement. Make the outer-border strips from the alphabet fabric. Alphabets are usually arranged in five rows of five or six letters. To make the border for a quilt you need four rows. Carefully position your ruler to give you the most seam allowance above and below each row of letters. Cut the rows apart and then determine where to cut the letters apart to create four approximately even-length strips. In the photographed quilt, I used six letters for the top and bottom borders and seven letters for the side borders. Each border strip required patches of off-white fabric to complete the necessary length as a border. Piece the border strips together, and then determine how much additional length is needed to make two border strips for each of the measurements you noted earlier. For each border strip, cut a piece of the off-white fabric that matches the background of the alphabet fabric the same width as the border strip and the length required plus ½". Cut this piece in half and add each half to the ends of the strip.

4. Sew the side border strips to the sides of the quilt top. From the remainder of the red fabric, cut four squares that measure the same as the width of the top and bottom border strips. For example, if your border strips were cut 4¾" wide, cut four 4¾" squares. Sew a square to each end of the top and bottom border strips. Sew these borders to the top and bottom edges of the quilt top.

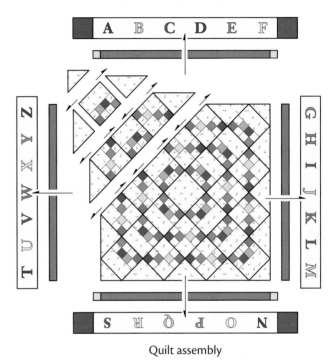

Quilt assembly

finishing the quilt

Refer to "Quilting ABCs," beginning with "Preparing to Quilt" on page 14, for more details on quilting and finishing.

1. Cut the backing fabric so it is approximately 4" to 6" larger than the quilt top.

2. Layer the backing, batting, and quilt top, and baste the layers together.

3. Hand or machine quilt as desired. The quilt shown was machine quilted with a loop-within-a-loop design in the background space between each row of blocks. A wavy line was quilted in the inner border, and the outer border was quilted with another loopy design.

4. Trim the batting and backing fabric so the edges are even with the quilt-top edges. Add a hanging sleeve, if desired. Bind the quilt edges, but use a ½"-wide seam allowance to create a wider binding.

The sweet colors of the 1930s-style fabrics and the mischievous prairie-point flags give this quilt its friendly charm. Wide cheerful little tents are sure to bring out a smile when you lay Baby on this quilt. The three-dimensional flags will add much tactile pleasure for Baby.

tiny TENTS

materials

Yardages are based on 42"-wide fabric.

1 yard of aqua print for background and outer border

¼ yard of white tone-on-tone print for blocks

¼ yard *each* of pink, blue, yellow, and lavender prints for blocks and inner border

⅜ yard of fabric for binding

1 yard of fabric for backing

34" x 34" square of batting

cutting

From *each* of the pink, blue, yellow, and lavender prints, cut:
1 strip, 2" x 42" (4 total)
1 square, 3" x 3" (4 total)
1 strip, 1½" x 21" (4 total)
1 rectangle, 2" x 7½" (4 total)
1 rectangle, 1½" x 4" (4 total)

From the white tone-on-tone print, cut:
2 strips, 1½" x 42"; crosscut each strip in half to make 4 strips, 1½" x 21"

From the aqua print, cut:
1 strip, 7½" x 42"; crosscut into 4 squares, 7½" x 7½"
2 strips, 4" x 42"; crosscut into 12 squares, 4" x 4"
4 strips, 3¾" x 42"

From the fabric for binding, cut:
4 strips, 2½" x 42"

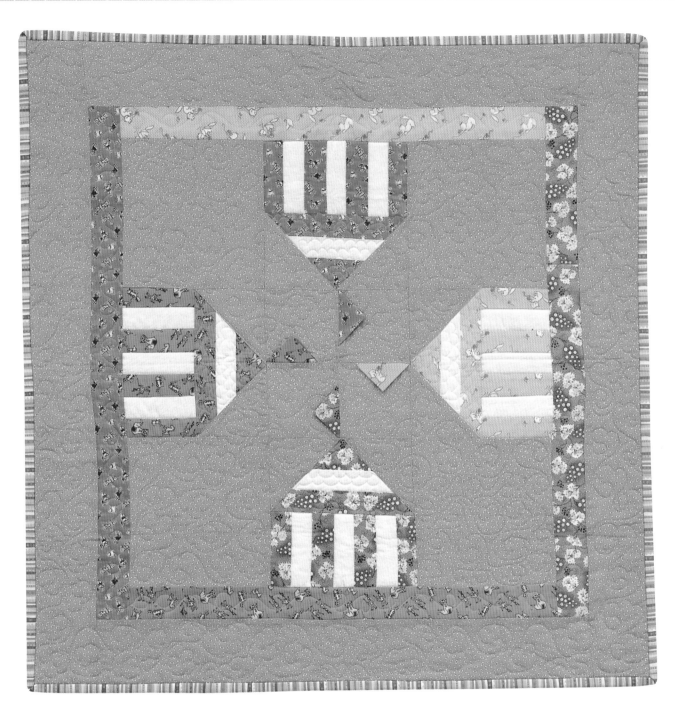

Designed and pieced by Mary Hickey. Quilted by Julie Goodwin.
Quilt size: 30½" x 30½" • Block size: 7" x 7"

making the tent blocks

1. Stitch the pink 1½" x 21" strip to a white 1½" x 21" strip to make a strip set. Repeat with the blue, yellow, and lavender strips. Crosscut each strip set into one segment, 7½" wide, and three segments, 4" wide.

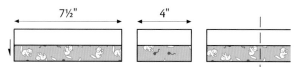

Make 1 strip set each of pink, blue, yellow, and lavender.
Cut each strip set into 1 segment, 7½" wide,
and 3 segments, 4" wide.

2. Sew the matching print 2" x 7½" rectangle to the white strip side of each 7½"-wide segment from step 1.

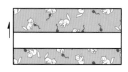

3. Stitch the three 4"-wide segments from each strip set together side by side so the colors alternate. Add the matching print 1½" x 4" rectangle to the end of each unit. Be sure the finished units measure 7½" wide.

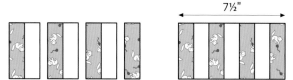

4. Sew the units from step 2 to the top of the matching units from step 3.

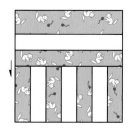

5. Using a pencil and rotary-cutting ruler, draw a diagonal line from corner to corner on the wrong side of eight aqua 4" squares. Refer to "Folded Corners" on page 12 to place a marked square on the upper corners of each unit from step 4. Sew on the marked lines, trim ¼" from the stitching lines, flip the aqua triangles open, and press.

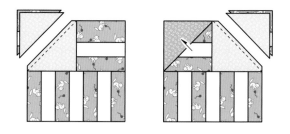

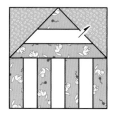

making the flag block

1. Fold each print 3" square in half, wrong sides together, and then fold the sides to the middle as shown to make the prairie point flags.

2. With the folded edges face down, sandwich the lavender flag between two aqua 4" squares so that the side point is flush with the square upper raw edges. Sew the squares together along the flag long edge. Repeat with the blue flag.

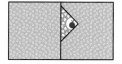

TINY TENTS
54

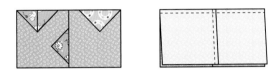

3. Position the pink and yellow flags on the purple flag rectangle as shown, being sure the flag tips are flush with the rectangle outer edges. Lay the blue flag rectangle over the purple flag rectangle so that the blue and purple flags are on the same edge. Sew the rectangles together. Press the block so that the flag open edges are down.

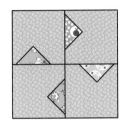

assembling the quilt top

1. Refer to the quilt assembly diagram to arrange the blocks and aqua 7½" squares into three rows of three blocks each. Sew the squares in each row together, and then sew the rows together.

2. Refer to "Adding Borders" on page 13 to measure the quilt top for borders. Sew the yellow and pink 2"-wide inner-border strips to the top and bottom edges of the quilt top, and then sew the blue and purple 2"-wide inner-border strips to the sides of the quilt top. Repeat with the aqua 3¾"-wide outer-border strips.

finishing the quilt

Refer to "Quilting ABCs," beginning with "Preparing to Quilt" on page 14, for more details on quilting and finishing.

1. Cut the backing fabric so it is approximately 4" to 6" larger than the quilt top.

2. Layer the backing, batting, and quilt top and baste the layers together.

3. Hand or machine quilt as desired. The quilt shown was machine quilted in the ditch in the tent blocks and with a scallop design on the roofs. The rest of the quilt was quilted in a meandering design.

4. Trim the batting and backing fabric so the edges are even with the quilt-top edges. Attach a hanging sleeve, if desired, and then bind the quilt. Add a label.

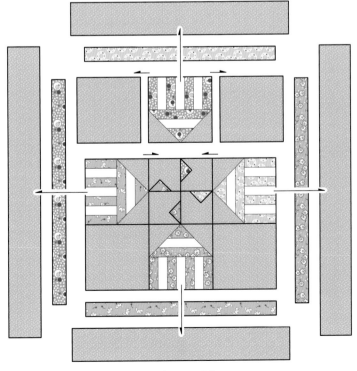

Quilt assembly

A traditional red-white-and-blue color scheme gives this quilt much of its energy. By making the noses and tails of the airplanes with prairie points, we eliminate much of the difficulty. Use the templates on page 61 to cut the airplane body and its background pieces and use your rotary cutter to slice out the other pieces.

airPLANES

materials

Yardages are based on 42"-wide fabric.

1³⁄₈ yards of white print for background

⁷⁄₈ yard of red print for alternate blocks and inner border

³⁄₄ yard of blue print for outer border

¹⁄₂ yard *total* of assorted blue prints for airplanes

¹⁄₂ yard of dark blue print for binding

2⁷⁄₈ yards of fabric for backing

46" x 63" piece of batting

Template plastic or lightweight cardboard

cutting

The patterns for templates A and B are on page 61.

From the assorted blue prints, cut 8 sets of pieces, with each set cut from the same fabric and consisting of:
2 squares, 3" x 3" (16 total)
1 rectangle, 2" x 6½" (D) (8 total)
1 template B piece (8 total)

From the white print, cut:
2 strips, 4" x 42". Fold the strips in half. Using template A, cut out 8 A and 8 A reversed pieces. By keeping the strips folded, you will be cutting 1 A piece and 1 A reversed piece each time you cut.

2 strips, 2½" x 42"; crosscut into 8 rectangles, 2½" x 6½" (C)

3 strips, 1½" x 42"; crosscut into 16 rectangles, 1½" x 6½" (E and F)

5 strips, 2" x 42"; crosscut into 16 rectangles, 2" x 9½" (G)

2 strips, 5" x 42"; crosscut into:

    2 rectangles, 5" x 9½"

    8 squares, 5" x 5"

3 strips, 2¾" x 42"; crosscut 1 strip into 4 rectangles, 2¾" x 5"

Designed and pieced by Mary Hickey. Quilted by Dawn Kelly.

Quilt size: 39" x 57" • Blocks size: 9" x 9"

From the red print, cut:
7 strips, 2¾" x 42"

1 square, 5" x 5"

4 squares, 2¾" x 2¾"

From the blue print for outer border, cut:
5 strips, 4¼" x 42"

From the dark blue print for binding, cut:
6 strips, 2½" x 42"

making the airplane blocks

1. Fold each blue 3" square in half, wrong sides together, and then fold the sides to the middle as shown to make the prairie points for the nose and tail of the airplanes.

2. Fold each blue D rectangle in half so the short ends meet and press a crease to mark the center.

3. Using matching blue pieces, center a prairie point, folded side up, on a D rectangle, with the straight edge of the prairie point aligned with the top of the rectangle and the point aligned with the center crease. Place the white C rectangle over the D rectangle and prairie point, right sides together. Stitch along the long top edge of the rectangles. Repeat to make a total of eight nose/wing units. Do not press the units yet.

Crease

4. Fold the B pieces in half along the top straight edge and press a crease to mark the center. Sew an A and an A reversed piece to each side of the B pieces to make the airplane body units.

Crease

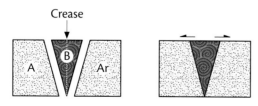

5. With the center creases aligned, stitch each body unit to its matching nose/wing unit. Press the seam allowances toward the D rectangles and the prairie points toward the C rectangles.

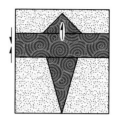

6. Fold the white E and F rectangles in half so the short ends meet and press a crease to mark the centers. Center a prairie point, folded side down, on each E rectangle, aligning the long straight edge of the prairie point with the bottom edge of the rectangle and the point with the center crease. Place an F rectangle over each of these pieces, right sides together, aligning the long edges along the bottom of the wider rectangle. Sew the pieces together to make the tail units.

Crease

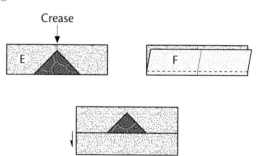

7. Stitch each tail unit to its matching body unit, centering the point of the prairie point with the tip of the body. Be careful not to catch the point of the prairie point in the seam allowance.

8. Sew a white G rectangle to the sides of each airplane unit.

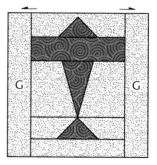

Make 8.

making the alternate blocks

1. Sew a white 2¾" x 42" strip to a red 2¾" strip to make a strip set. Repeat to make a total of two strip sets. Crosscut the strip sets into 24 segments, 2¾" wide.

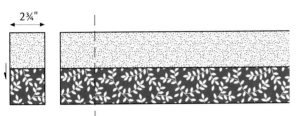

Make 2 strip sets.
Cut 24 segments.

2. Sew two segments together to make a four-patch unit. Repeat to make a total of 12 units.

Make 12.

3. Sew two four-patch units and two white 5" squares together to make block A. Repeat to make a total of four blocks.

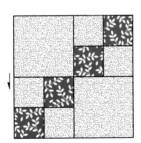

Block A.
Make 4.

4. Sew two four-patch units and a white 5" x 9½" rectangle together to make block B. Repeat to make a total of two blocks.

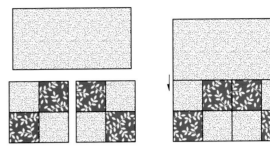

Block B.
Make 2.

5. Sew the red 2¾" squares, the white 2¾" x 5" rectangles, and the red 5" square together to make block C.

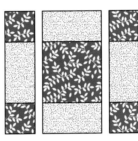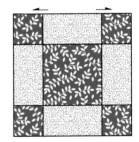

Block C.
Make 1.

assembling the quilt top

1. Refer to the quilt assembly diagram to arrange the blocks into five rows of three blocks each. Make sure all the blocks are positioned correctly to create the pattern. Sew the blocks in each row together, and then sew the rows together.

2. Refer to "Adding Borders" on page 13 to measure the quilt top for borders. Sew the red print 2¾"-wide inner-border strips to the quilt top. Repeat with the blue print 4¼"-wide outer-border strips.

finishing the quilt

Refer to "Quilting ABCs," beginning with "Preparing to Quilt" on page 14, for more details on quilting and finishing.

1. Cut the backing fabric so it is approximately 4" to 6" larger than the quilt top.

2. Layer the backing, batting, and quilt top and baste the layers together.

3. Hand or machine quilt as desired. The quilt shown was machine quilted with a zigzag pattern on the airplane wings and filled in with an allover swirl design. The borders were quilted with a repeating wave design.

4. Trim the batting and backing fabric so the edges are even with the quilt-top edges. Attach a hanging sleeve, if desired, and then bind the quilt. Add a label.

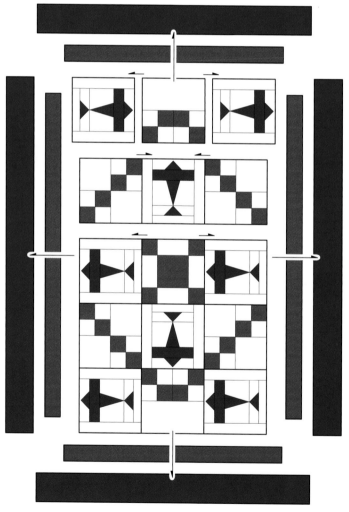

Quilt assembly

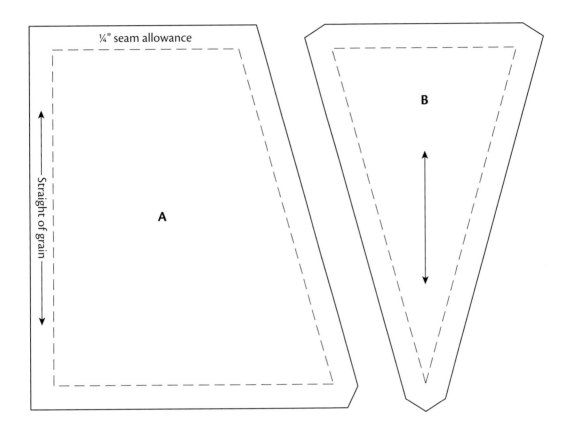

¼" seam allowance

Straight of grain

A

B

This quilt provides an excellent way to use a small conversation print. The tiny triangles on the corners of the sailboat squares are easy to piece using folded corners; the other four triangles are cleverly fashioned from prairie points.

gift BLOCK

materials

Yardages are based on 42"-wide fabric.

²/₃ yard of blue bubble print for sashing rectangles and inner border

⅝ yard of beach print for outer border

½ yard of white tone-on-tone print for blocks

½ yard of sailboat print for blocks

¼ yard *each* of blue, purple, and yellow prints for blocks and sashing squares

³/₈ yard of fabric for binding

1¼ yards of fabric for backing

42" x 42" square of batting

cutting

From the sailboat print, fussy cut:
9 squares, 4" x 4"

From the white tone-on-tone print, cut:
6 strips, 2" x 42"; crosscut into:
   18 rectangles, 2" x 4"
   18 rectangles, 2" x 7"

From the yellow print, cut:
1 strip, 2¼" x 42"; crosscut into 12 squares, 2¼" x 2¼"
12 squares, 1¼" x 1¼"
4 squares, 3" x 3"

From *each* of the blue and purple prints, cut:
1 strip, 1¼" x 42"; crosscut into 12 squares, 1¼" x 1¼"
   (24 total)
1 strip, 2¼" x 42"; crosscut into 12 squares, 2¼" x 2¼"
   (24 total)

From the blue bubble print, cut:
7 strips, 3" x 42"; crosscut 3 strips into
   12 rectangles, 3" x 7"

From the beach print, cut:
4 strips, 4¼" x 42"

From the fabric for binding, cut:
4 strips, 2½" x 42"

Designed and pieced by Cleo Nollette. Quilted by Julie Goodwin.

Quilt size: 37" x 37" • Block size: 6½" x 6½"

making the gift blocks

1. Using a pencil and rotary-cutting ruler, draw a diagonal line from corner to corner on the wrong side of each blue, purple, and yellow 1¼" square. Refer to "Folded Corners" on page 12 to place matching squares on the corners of each sailboat print square. Sew on the marked lines, trim ¼" from the stitching lines, flip the triangles open, and press.

Make 3 blue, 3 purple, and 3 yellow.

2. Fold each of the blue, yellow, and purple 2¼" squares in half, wrong sides together. Fold the corners to the middle, overlapping the edges about ¼" to make the prairie point.

3. Center a prairie point that matches the corner squares on each side of the unit from step 1, with the folds facing up and the points aiming toward the center of the unit. Overlap the corner triangles by about ¼". Baste the prairie points in place.

4. Sew the white 2" x 4" rectangles to the top and bottom of each sailboat square. Press the seam allowances toward the center of the units and the prairie points toward the rectangles.

5. Stitch the white 2" x 7" rectangles to the sides of each sailboat square. Press the seam allowances toward the center of the blocks and the prairie points toward the rectangles.

Make 9.

assembling the quilt top

1. Refer to the quilt assembly diagram to alternately arrange the blocks and blue bubble print 3" x 7" rectangles into three rows of three blocks and two rectangles each. Stitch the blocks and rectangles in each row together to make the block rows.

2. Alternately sew three blue bubble print 3" x 7" rectangles and two yellow 3" squares together to make a sashing row. Repeat to make a total of two sashing rows.

3. Alternately sew the block rows and sashing rows together.

4. Refer to "Adding Borders" on page 13 to measure the quilt top for borders. Sew the blue bubble print 3"-wide inner-border strips to the quilt top. Repeat for the beach print 4¼"-wide outer-border strips.

finishing the quilt

Refer to "Quilting ABCs," beginning with "Preparing to Quilt" on page 14, for more details on quilting and finishing.

1. Cut the backing fabric so it is approximately 4" to 6" larger than the quilt top.

2. Layer the backing, batting, and quilt top and baste the layers together.

3. Hand or machine quilt as desired. The quilt shown was machine quilted in the ditch in the blocks and with waves and vines in the sashing and borders.

4. Trim the batting and backing fabric so the edges are even with the quilt-top edges. Attach a hanging sleeve, if desired, and then bind the quilt. Add a label.

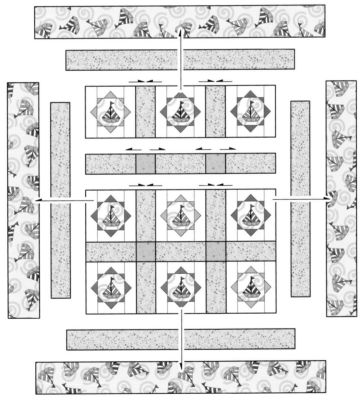

Quilt assembly

baby bows and TWINKLE TOES

Nothing reminds me of my own babyhood faster than the sight of shiny new Mary Janes. These tiny shoes skip between the bows and dance across the quilt top. They are a breeze to fuse to the background, and you can stitch them with a straight, zigzag, or blanket stitch.

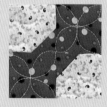

materials

Yardages are based on 42"-wide fabric.

¾ yard *total* of assorted white-and-red prints for background

⅓ yard *total* of assorted red prints for bow ties and shoe linings

½ yard of red print for outer border

⅓ yard of white-and-red striped fabric for inner border

¼ yard of black print for shoes

⅜ yard of fabric for binding

1¼ yards of fabric for backing

40" x 40" square of batting

½ yard of paper-backed fusible web

cutting

From the assorted red prints, cut *8 sets* of pieces, with each set cut from the same fabric and consisting of:
2 squares, 2½" x 2½" (16 total)
2 squares, 1½" x 1½" (16 total)

From the assorted white-and-red prints, cut a *total* of:
17 squares, 5½" x 5½"

8 pairs of matching squares, 2½" x 2½" (16 total)

From the remainder of the assorted white-and-red prints, cut *8 sets* of pieces, with each set cut from the same fabric and consisting of:
1 rectangle, 1½" x 4½" (8 total)
1 rectangle, 1½" x 5½" (8 total)

From the white-and-red striped fabric, cut:
4 strips, 2" x 42"

From the red print for outer border, cut:
4 strips, 4" x 42"

From the fabric for binding, cut:
4 strips, 2½" x 42"

Designed, pieced, and appliquéd by Mary Hickey. Quilted by Dawn Kelly.

Quilt size: 35" x 35" • Blocks size: 5" x 5"

making the bow tie blocks

1. Using a pencil and rotary-cutting ruler, draw a diagonal line from corner to corner on the wrong side of each assorted red 1½" square. Refer to "Folded Corners" on page 12 to place a square on one corner of each assorted white-and-red print 2½" square. Sew on the marked lines, trim ¼" from the stitching lines, flip the triangles open, and press.

2. Sew two matching squares from step 1 and the two matching assorted red print 2½" squares from the same set together to make a bow-tie unit. Add an assorted white-and-red print 1½" x 4½" rectangle to the right side of the unit and the matching 1½" x 5½" rectangle to the bottom of the unit to complete the block. Repeat to make a total of eight Bow Tie blocks.

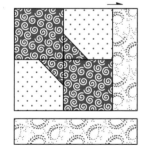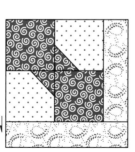

Make 8.

assembling the quilt top

1. Refer to the quilt assembly diagram to arrange the blocks and assorted white-and-red 5½" squares into five rows, positioning the Bow Tie blocks in the directions shown. Sew the squares in each row together, and then sew the rows together.

2. Refer to "Adding Borders" on page 13 to measure the quilt top for borders. Sew the white-and-red striped 2"-wide inner-border strips to the quilt top. Repeat for the red print 4"-wide outer-border strips.

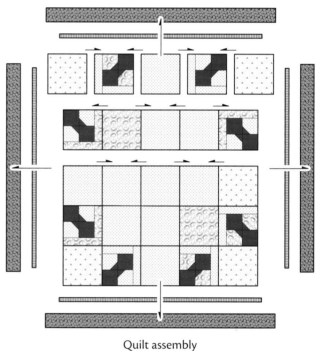

Quilt assembly

3. Refer to "Fusible Appliqué" on page 12 to make the shoe and shoe lining appliqué shapes on page 69 and appliqué them to the quilt top. Refer to the photo on page 67 for placement as needed. Stitch around the shapes by hand or machine using a straight, zigzag, or blanket stitch.

finishing the quilt

Refer to "Quilting ABCs," beginning with "Preparing to Quilt" on page 14, for more details on quilting and finishing.

1. Cut the backing fabric so it is approximately 4" to 6" larger than the quilt top.

2. Layer the backing, batting, and quilt top and baste the layers together.

3. Hand or machine quilt as desired. The quilt shown was machine quilted with scrolled feathers through the blocks and spirals in the borders.

4. Trim the batting and backing fabric so the edges are even with the quilt-top edges. Attach a hanging sleeve, if desired, and then bind the quilt. Add a label.

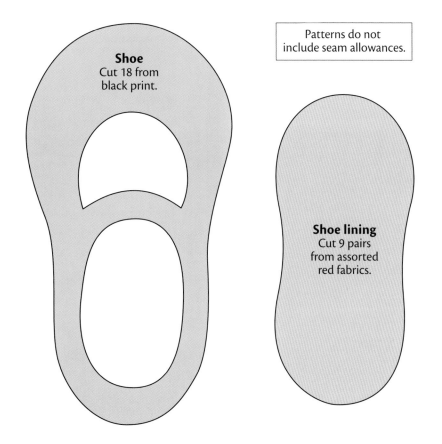

Shoe
Cut 18 from
black print.

Patterns do not
include seam allowances.

Shoe lining
Cut 9 pairs
from assorted
red fabrics.

My own cat posed for the drawings of these happy little kittens. Their large, fluffy shapes are easy to cut and stitch. You can make your cats out of any colors you choose. While mine are blondes, yours can be marmalade, or tabby, or even purple. After fusing mine, I stitched them down with two or three lines of straight stitches in a thread color darker than the fabric color to give definition to their shapes.

cozy KITTENS

materials

Yardages are based on 42"-wide fabric.

2/3 yard of light blue print for block backgrounds

5/8 yard of medium blue print for outer border

1/2 yard of beige print for sashing and inner border

1/4 yard *total* of 4 or 5 assorted tan prints for cats

6" x 8" rectangle of orange print for goldfish

Scraps of yellow, red, and blue prints for star, ball, and bird

3/8 yard of fabric for binding

1 1/3 yards of fabric for backing

35" x 45" piece of batting

1 yard of paper-backed fusible web

Dark tan and black topstitching threads

Sewing-machine topstitching needle

Black embroidery floss (optional)

Black fine-line permanent marker (optional)

cutting

From the light blue print, cut:
1 strip, 11" x 42"; crosscut into:
    2 rectangles, 8 1/2" x 11"
    2 rectangles, 9" x 11"
1 strip, 9" x 42"; crosscut into:
    1 rectangle, 6" x 9"
    1 square, 9" x 9"

From the beige print, cut:
6 strips, 2 1/2" x 42"; crosscut *1* strip into:
    2 rectangles, 2 1/2" x 9"
    2 rectangles, 2 1/2" x 11"

From the medium blue print, cut:
4 strips, 4 1/4" x 42"

From the fabric for binding, cut:
4 strips, 2 1/2" x 42"

Designed, pieced, and appliquéd by Mary Hickey. Quilted by Dawn Kelly
Quilt size: 30" x 40"

assembling the blocks

1. Refer to "Fusible Appliqué" on page 12 to make the five cat appliqué shapes and the fish, ball, and bird appliqué shapes on pages 73–79. Refer to the quilt assembly diagram at right to apply each shape to the center of the appropriate blue print square or rectangle. Machine straight stitch around each shape two or three times using the tan topstitching thread and the topstitching needle. Be sure to stitch the detail lines as shown on the pattern by the broken lines.

2. Using a zigzag stitch and black topstitching thread, machine stitch the eyes and noses on the cats, fish, and bird, or hand embroider them using a satin stitch and black embroidery floss.

3. Draw the mouths on each cat with the permanent marker, or hand embroider them using a back-stitch or stem stitch and black embroidery floss.

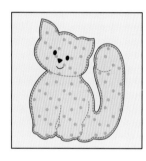

assembling the quilt top

1. Refer to the quilt assembly diagram to arrange the blocks and beige print 2½" x 9" and 2½" x 11" sashing rectangles into two vertical rows of three blocks and two sashing rectangles each. Sew the blocks and sashing rectangles in each row together.

2. Measure the block rows through the vertical center. The two measurements should be the same; if not, check your seam allowances and make adjustments as needed. Trim three of the remaining beige print 2½" x 42" strips to this measurement. Alternately sew the beige strips and block rows together.

3. Measure the quilt top through the horizontal center and trim the remaining two beige print 2½" x 42" strips to this measurement. Sew the strips to the top and bottom edges of the quilt top.

4. Refer to "Adding Borders" on page 13 to measure the quilt top for the outer borders. Sew the medium blue 4¼"-wide strips to the quilt top.

Quilt assembly

finishing the quilt

Refer to "Quilting ABCs," beginning with "Preparing to Quilt" on page 14, for more details on quilting and finishing.

1. Cut the backing fabric so it is approximately 4" to 6" larger than the quilt top.

2. Layer the backing, batting, and quilt top, and baste the layers together.

3. Hand or machine quilt as desired. The quilt shown was machine quilted with an allover design in the block background, lighthearted loops and curves in the sashing and inner border, and balls of yarn in the outer border.

4. Trim the batting and backing fabric so the edges are even with the quilt-top edges. Attach a hanging sleeve, if desired, and then bind the quilt. Add a label.

Stitching details

Top-left cat
Cut 1 from assorted tan prints.

Pattern does not include seam allowance
and has been reversed for fusible appliqué.

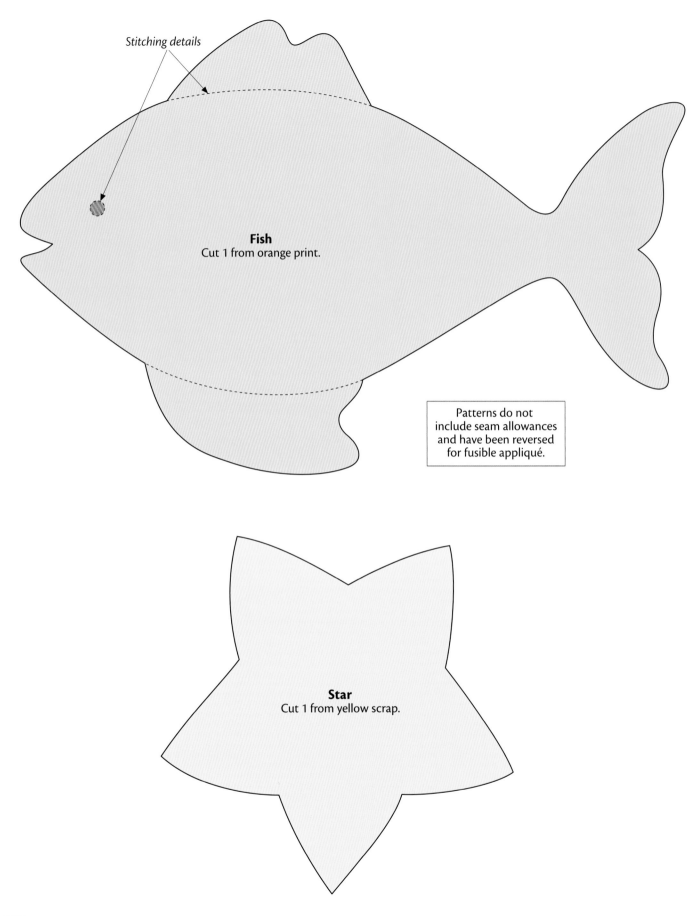

Stitching details

Fish
Cut 1 from orange print.

Patterns do not
include seam allowances
and have been reversed
for fusible appliqué.

Star
Cut 1 from yellow scrap.

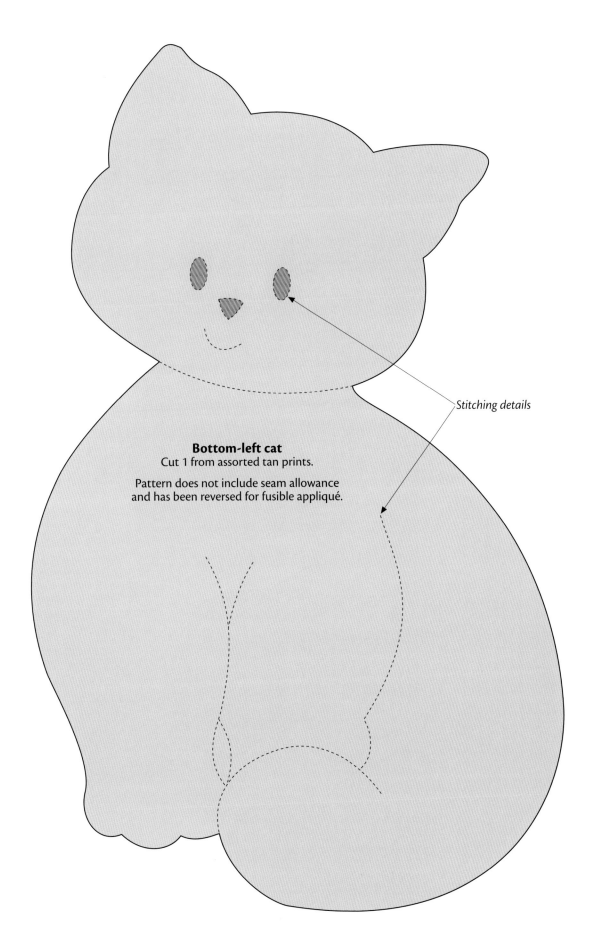

Stitching details

Bottom-left cat
Cut 1 from assorted tan prints.

Pattern does not include seam allowance
and has been reversed for fusible appliqué.

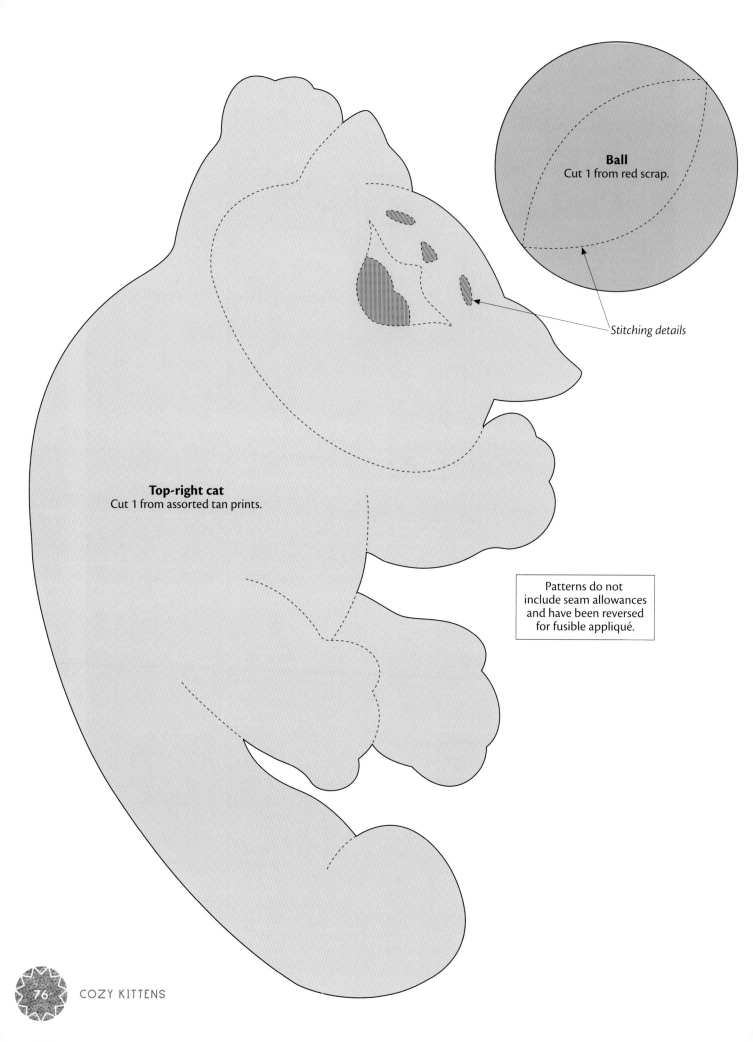

Ball
Cut 1 from red scrap.

Stitching details

Top-right cat
Cut 1 from assorted tan prints.

Patterns do not
include seam allowances
and have been reversed
for fusible appliqué.

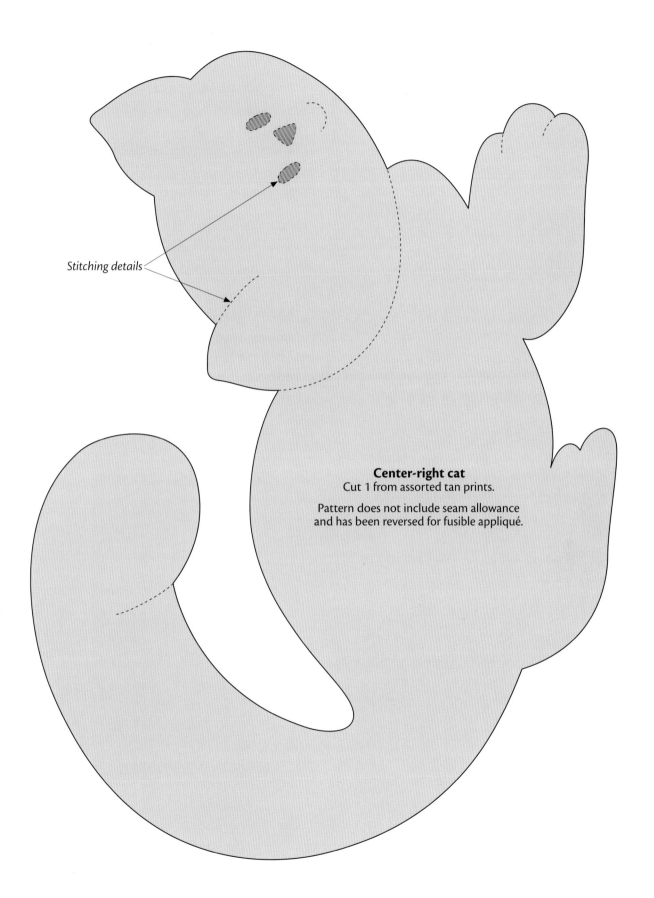

Stitching details

Center-right cat
Cut 1 from assorted tan prints.

Pattern does not include seam allowance
and has been reversed for fusible appliqué.

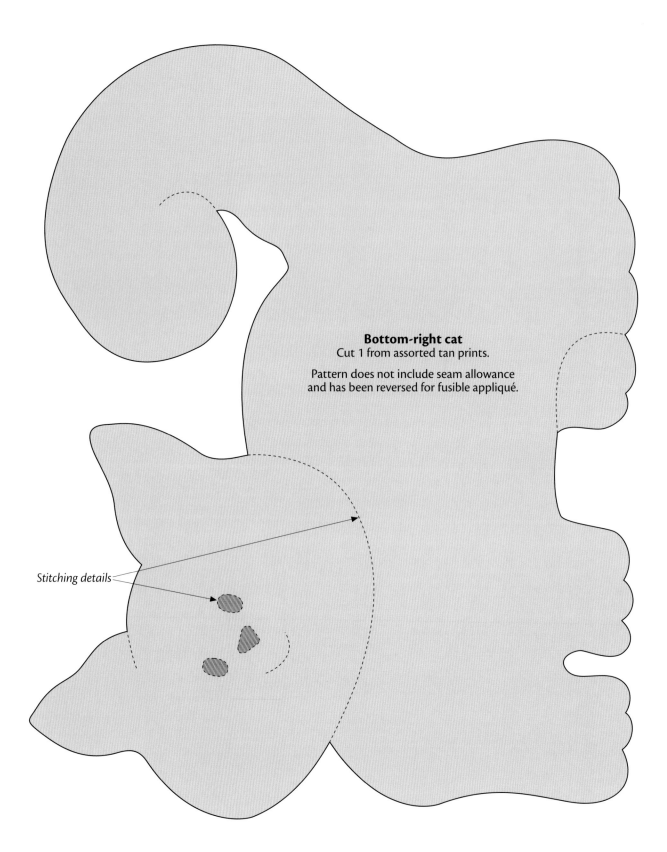

Bottom-right cat
Cut 1 from assorted tan prints.

Pattern does not include seam allowance
and has been reversed for fusible appliqué.

Stitching details

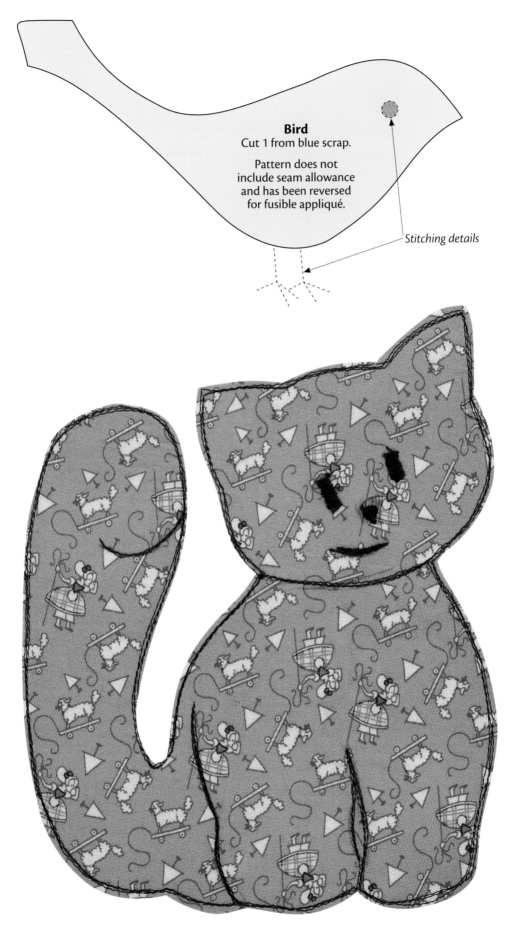

Bird
Cut 1 from blue scrap.

Pattern does not
include seam allowance
and has been reversed
for fusible appliqué.

Stitching details

The first colors of spring are always soft and subtle. Here in the Northwest, these subtle greens are always viewed through a mist of rain. Delicate greens and soft blues create a soothing wash of colors in this appealing quilt made of a simple pieced block. The light misty greens and the subtle blues blend together to create a graceful and soothing quilt. By making the quilt with scraps, you can add interest and translucency to the blocks.

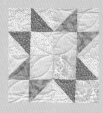

spring MIST

materials

Yardages are based on 42"-wide fabric.

¾ yard *total* of assorted light blue prints for blocks

¾ yard *total* of assorted light green prints for blocks

⅝ yard of medium blue print for outer border

⅓ yard of light blue print for inner border

¼ yard *total* of assorted medium blue prints for blocks

¼ yard *total* of assorted medium green prints for blocks

½ yard of fabric for binding

1¾ yards of fabric for backing

45" x 45" square of batting

cutting

From *each* of 1 assorted light blue and 1 assorted light green print, cut:
2 squares, 5½" x 5½" (4 total)

From *total* of the assorted light blue and light green prints, cut:
16 pairs of matching squares of each color, 3" x 3" (32 of each color; 64 total)
16 squares of each color, 3½" x 3½" (32 total)

From the assorted medium blue and medium green prints, cut:
16 squares of each color, 3½" x 3½" (32 total)

From the light blue print for inner border, cut:
4 strips, 2" x 42"

From the medium blue print for outer border, cut:
4 strips, 4" x 42"

From the fabric for binding, cut:
5 strips, 2½" x 42"

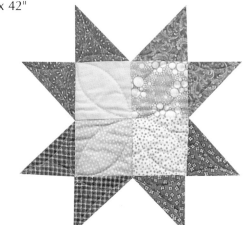

Designed and pieced by Mary Hickey. Quilted by Dawn Kelly.

Quilt size: 40" x 40" • Block size: 5" x 5"

making the blocks

1. Layer each light blue 3½" square with a medium blue 3½" square, right sides together, with the light blue square on top. Using a pencil and a rotary-cutting ruler, draw a diagonal line from corner to corner on the wrong side of the light blue squares. Stitch ¼" from each side of the marked line. Cut the squares apart on the marked line to yield 32 half-square-triangle units. Repeat with the light green and medium green 3½" squares. Trim each unit to 3" x 3".

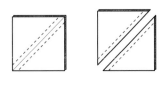

Make 32.   Make 32.

2. Sew together two matching blue half-square-triangle units and two matching light blue 3" squares. Repeat to make a total of 16 blue blocks. Repeat with the green half-square-triangle units and light green 3" squares to make a total of 16 green blocks.

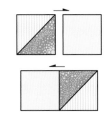

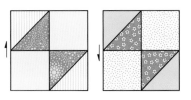

Make 16.   Make 16.

assembling the quilt top

1. Refer to the quilt assembly diagram to arrange the blocks and the light blue and light green 5½" squares into six rows of six blocks each. Be sure the blocks are oriented as shown. Sew the pieces in each row together, and then sew the rows together.

2. Refer to "Adding Borders" on page 13 to measure the quilt top for borders. Sew the light blue 2"-wide inner-border strips to the quilt top. Repeat for the medium blue 4"-wide outer-border strips.

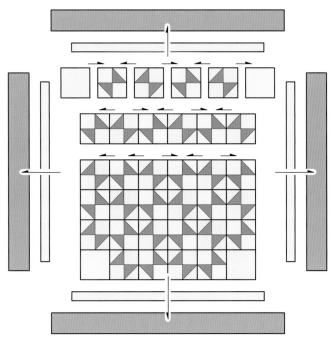

Quilt assembly

finishing the quilt

Refer to "Quilting ABCs," beginning with "Preparing to Quilt" on page 14, for more details on quilting and finishing.

1. Cut the backing fabric so it is approximately 4" to 6" larger than the quilt top.

2. Layer the backing, batting, and quilt top and baste the layers together.

3. Hand or machine quilt as desired. The quilt shown was machine quilted with a leaf shape and spirals in the blocks, a back and forth squiggly line in the inner border, and a spiral design in the outer border.

4. Trim the batting and backing fabric so the edges are even with the quilt-top edges. Attach a hanging sleeve, if desired, and then bind the quilt. Add a label.

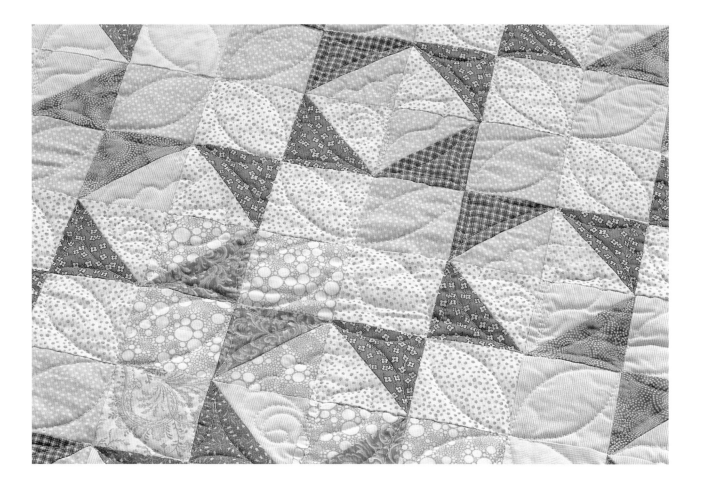

This beloved old block, the
Churn Dash, has always been
one of my favorites. I have
made it many times for gift
quilts, but I think I like it
made in these primary colors
the best. The striped fabric
used as sashing creates both
the energy in the quilt and the
color scheme for the blocks.
This cheerful quilt will add
a bright spot to any
baby's room.

binky SQUARES

materials

Yardages are based on 42"-wide fabric.

¾ yard of white tone-on-tone print for blocks

¾ yard of green print for blocks and outer border

⅝ yard of multicolored striped fabric for sashing
rectangles and inner border

⅓ yard of blue print for blocks and sashing squares

⅓ yard of red print for blocks and sashing squares

¼ yard of yellow print for blocks and sashing squares

⅛ yard of light blue print for blocks

⅛ yard of light red print for blocks

⅛ yard of light green print for blocks

⅛ yard of light yellow print for blocks

½ yard of fabric for binding

1½ yards of fabric for backing

38" x 50" piece of batting

cutting

From the white tone-on-tone print, cut:

4 strips, 3" x 42"; crosscut into 48 squares, 3" x 3"

7 strips, 1½" x 42"; crosscut 5 strips in half to yield
    10 strips, 1½" x 21"

From *each* of the light blue and light red prints, cut:

2 strips, 1½" x 42"; crosscut 1 strip in half to yield 2
    strips, 1½" x 21"

**From *each* of the light green and light yellow prints,
cut:**

2 strips, 1½" x 42"; cut in half to yield 4 strips,
    1½" x 21" (you will have 1 half strip left over)

From the blue print, cut:

2 strips, 3" x 42"; crosscut into 16 squares, 3" x 3"

1 strip, 1½" x 42"; crosscut into 12 squares, 1½" x 1½".
    Set aside the remainder of the strip for the strip set.

From the red print, cut:

2 strips, 3" x 42"; crosscut into 14 squares, 3" x 3"

1 strip, 1½" x 42"; crosscut into 10 squares, 1½" x 1½".
    Set aside the remainder of the strip for the strip set.

Designed and pieced by Mary Hickey. Quilted by Dawn Kelly.

Quilt size: 32½" x 44½" • Block size: 5" x 5"

From the green print, cut:

1 strip, 3" x 42"; crosscut into 12 squares, 3" x 3"

1 strip, 1½" x 42"; crosscut into 9 squares, 1½" x 1½".
  Set aside the remainder of the strip for the strip set.

4 strips, 4¼" x 42"

From the yellow print, cut:

1 strip, 3" x 42"; crosscut into 6 squares, 3" x 3"

1 strip, 1½" x 42"; crosscut into 4 squares, 1½" x 1½".
  Set aside the remainder of the strip for the strip set.

From the multicolored striped fabric, cut:

3 strips, 5½" x 42"; crosscut into 58 rectangles,
  1½" x 5½". Cut each strip so the colors are in the
  same sequence on each strip.

From the fabric for binding, cut:

5 strips, 2½" x 42"

making the blocks

1. Sew a white and a light blue 1½" x 42" strip
   together to make a strip set. Repeat with the white
   and light red 1½" x 42" strips. Crosscut the strip
   sets into the number of 1½"-wide segments indicated. Using the 1½" x 21" strips, make strip sets
   from the white and light green strips and the white
   and light yellow strips. Crosscut the strip sets into
   the number of 1½"-wide segments indicated.

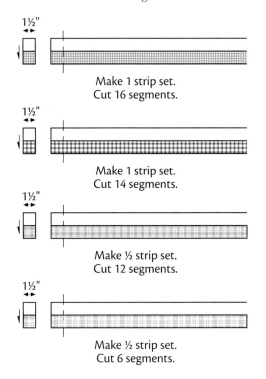

1½"

Make 1 strip set.
Cut 16 segments.

1½"

Make 1 strip set.
Cut 14 segments.

1½"

Make ½ strip set.
Cut 12 segments.

1½"

Make ½ strip set.
Cut 6 segments.

2. Using the white and light blue 1½" x 21" strips and
   the remainder of the blue 1½"-wide strip, make a strip
   set as shown. Make red, green, and yellow strip sets
   in the same manner. Crosscut each strip set into the
   number of 1½"-wide segments indicated.

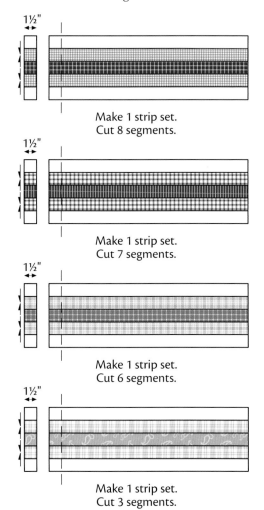

1½"

Make 1 strip set.
Cut 8 segments.

1½"

Make 1 strip set.
Cut 7 segments.

1½"

Make 1 strip set.
Cut 6 segments.

1½"

Make 1 strip set.
Cut 3 segments.

3. Layer each blue, red, green, and yellow 3" square
   with a white 3" square, right sides together, with the
   white square on top. Using a pencil and a rotary-
   cutting ruler, draw a diagonal line from corner to
   corner on the wrong side of the white squares.
   Stitch ¼" from each side of the marked line. Cut the
   squares apart on the marked line to yield 32 blue,
   28 red, 24 green, and 12 yellow half-square-triangle
   units. Trim each unit to 2½" x 2½".

Make 32.   Make 28.   Make 24.   Make 12.

4. Sew together four blue half-square-triangle units, two blue segments from step 1, and one blue segment from step 2 to make a blue block. Repeat to make a total of eight blocks. Repeat with the remaining units to make seven red blocks, six green blocks, and three yellow blocks.

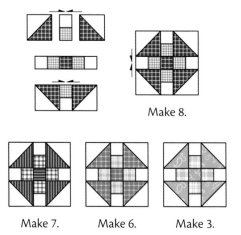

Make 8.

Make 7.   Make 6.   Make 3.

assembling the quilt top

1. Refer to the quilt assembly diagram to arrange the blocks and multicolored striped 1½" x 5½" sashing rectangles into six rows of four blocks and five sashing rectangles each. Pay careful attention to the color placement in each row. Sew the pieces in each row together.

Make 6 rows.

2. Refer to the quilt assembly diagram to arrange the 1½" squares and multicolored striped 1½" x 5½" sashing rectangles into seven rows of five squares and four sashing rectangles each. Again, pay careful attention to the color placement in each row. Sew the pieces in each row together.

Make 7 rows.

3. Sew the block rows and sashing rows together.

4. Refer to "Adding Borders" on page 13 to measure the quilt top for the border. Sew the green 4¼"-wide border strips to the quilt top.

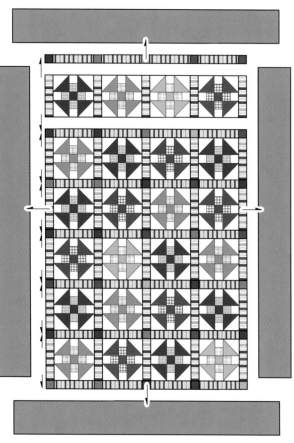

Quilt assembly

finishing the quilt

Refer to "Quilting ABCs," beginning with "Preparing to Quilt" on page 14, for more details on quilting and finishing.

1. Cut the backing fabric so it is approximately 4" to 6" larger than the quilt top.

2. Layer the backing, batting, and quilt top and baste the layers together.

3. Hand or machine quilt as desired. The quilt shown was machine quilted with allover spirals in the blocks and borders.

4. Trim the batting and backing fabric so the edges are even with the quilt-top edges. Attach a hanging sleeve, if desired, and then bind the quilt. Add a label.

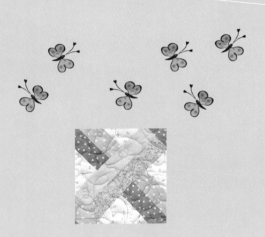

I love this remarkably clever little quilt—repeating one simple block magically creates the illusion of a trellis. This quilt is just the right size for the serious work of a baby quilt: cuddling, burping, drooling, and all-around comforting. And you can whip it up in a hurry, too. For best results, pick two shades of lime green and two shades of aqua, and remember to pin the seam intersections before stitching.

petite TRELLIS

materials

Yardages are based on 42"-wide fabric.

½ yard of blue butterfly print for outer border

⅓ yard of light blue print for blocks

⅓ yard of medium blue print for blocks

⅓ yard of white tone-on-tone print for blocks

¼ yard of light lime green print for blocks

¼ yard of medium lime green print for blocks

¼ yard of blue-and-lime-green striped fabric for inner border

⅜ yard of fabric for binding

1¼ yards of fabric for backing

34" x 40" piece of batting

Square rotary-cutting ruler

cutting

From *each* of the light blue and medium blue, cut:
4 strips, 1½" x 42"

1 strip, 2¼" x 42"; crosscut into 10 squares, 2¼" x 2¼".
   Cut each square once diagonally to yield 20 triangles.

From the white tone-on-tone print, cut:
2 strips, 4" x 42"; crosscut into 20 squares, 4" x 4". Cut
   each square twice diagonally to yield 80 triangles.

From *each* of the medium lime green and light lime green prints, cut:
4 strips, 1½" x 42"

From the blue-and-lime-green striped fabric, cut:
4 strips, 1" x 42"

From the blue butterfly print, cut:
4 strips, 3¼" x 42"

From the fabric for binding, cut:
4 strips, 2½" x 42"

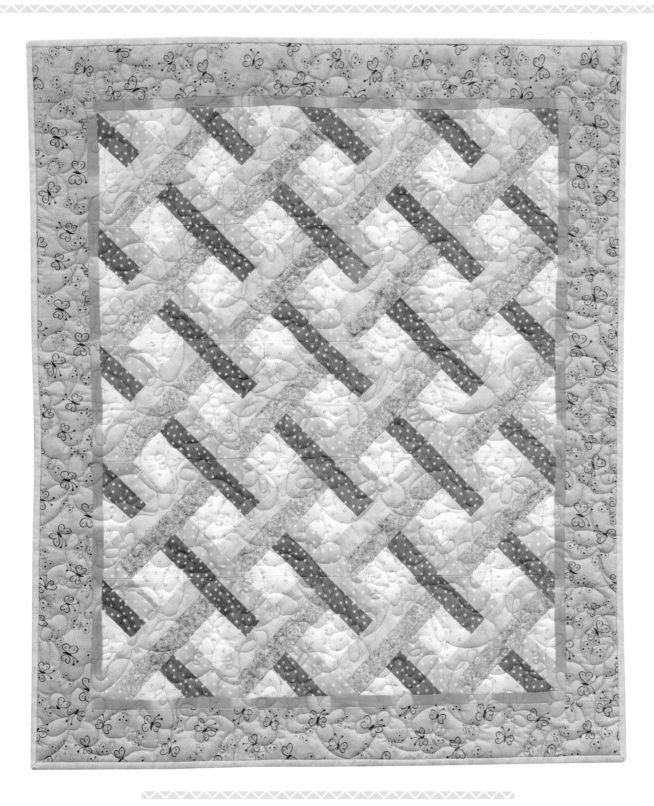

Designed by Mary Hickey. Pieced by Cleo Nollette. Quilted by Frankie Schmitt.

Quilt size: 29½" x 35¼" • Block size: 5¾" x 5¾"

making the trellis blocks

1. Sew each medium blue 1½" x 42" strip to a light blue 1½" x 42" strip to make four strip sets. Press the seam allowances open. Crosscut the strip sets into 20 segments, 7¼" wide.

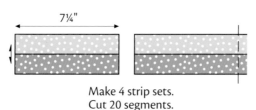

Make 4 strip sets.
Cut 20 segments.

2. Fold each segment in half crosswise, wrong sides together. Place your rotary-cutting ruler as close as possible to the folded edge; cut off the fold. With the trimmed pairs still layered, align the 45° angle of the square ruler with the seam line of the top segment and place the ruler corner just barely below the top of the segments. Cut along the angled edges of the ruler to create 20 pairs.

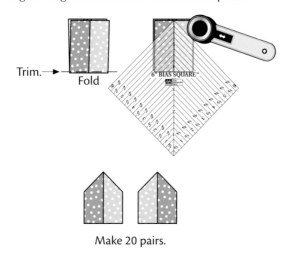

Make 20 pairs.

3. Sew a white triangle to the straight sides of each blue segment.

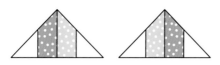

Make 20 of each.

4. Sew each medium lime green 1½" x 42" strip to a light lime green 1½" x 42" strip to make four strip sets. Crosscut the strip sets into 20 segments, 6⅝" wide.

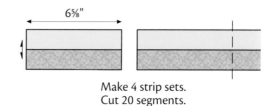

Make 4 strip sets.
Cut 20 segments.

5. Sew a light blue triangle and a medium blue triangle to each lime green segment as shown.

6. Sew together two blue units (make sure they are mirror images of each other) and one lime green unit to complete the block. Repeat to make a total of 20 blocks.

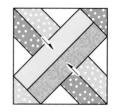

Make 20.

assembling the quilt top

1. Refer to the quilt assembly diagram to carefully arrange the blocks into five rows of four blocks each. The blocks must be positioned the same in each row in order for the trellis design to form. Carefully pin and sew the blocks in each row together, and then pin and sew the rows together.

2. Refer to "Adding Borders" on page 13 to measure the quilt top for borders. Sew the blue-and-lime-green striped 1"-wide inner-border strips to the quilt top. Repeat for the blue butterfly print 3¼"-wide outer-border strips.

finishing the quilt

Refer to "Quilting ABCs," beginning with "Preparing to Quilt" on page 14, for more details on quilting and finishing.

1. Cut the backing fabric so it is approximately 4" to 6" larger than the quilt top.

2. Layer the backing, batting, and quilt top and baste the layers together.

3. Hand or machine quilt as desired. The quilt shown was machine quilted with an allover floral and butterfly design.

4. Trim the batting and backing fabric so the edges are even with the quilt-top edges. Attach a hanging sleeve, if desired, and then bind the quilt. Add a label.

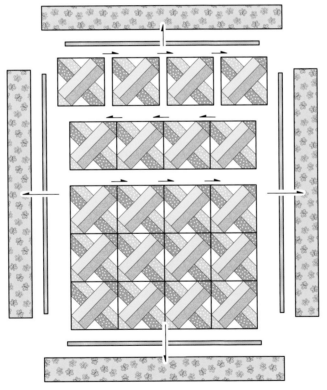

Quilt assembly

A sumptuous rainbow of color cascades from this beautiful little quilt. A light, medium, and dark value of each color is required, so you'll need an ample collection of scraps. I suggest you dig through your scraps and your friends' stashes for the colors you want, or purchase fat quarters and fat eighths in the needed colors.

over the RAINBOW

materials

Yardages are based on 42"-wide fabric.

1 yard of dark pink print for blocks, inner and outer borders, and binding

½ yard of light pink print for blocks and middle border

¼ yard of medium pink print for blocks

1 fat quarter *each* of light blue and light green prints

1 fat eighth *each* of dark blue and medium blue prints

1 fat eighth *each* of dark green and medium green prints

1 fat eighth *each* of dark aqua, medium aqua, and light aqua prints

1 fat eighth *each* of dark purple, medium purple, and light purple prints

1 fat eighth *each* of dark yellow, medium yellow, and light yellow prints

1⅓ yards of fabric for backing

42" x 42" square of batting

cutting

From the medium pink print, cut:
2 strips, 1¾" x 42"

From the light pink print, cut:
2 strips, 1¾" x 42"
1 strip, 3½" x 42"; crosscut into 8 squares, 3½" x 3½"
4 strips, 2½" x 42"

From the medium blue print, cut:
4 strips, 1¾" x 20"

From the light blue print, cut:
2 strips, 3½" x 20"; crosscut into 10 squares, 3½" x 3½"
4 strips, 1¾" x 20"

From the medium green print, cut:
3 strips, 1¾" x 20"

Designed and pieced by Mary Hickey. Quilted by Frankie Schmitt.
Quilt size: 38" x 38" • Block size: 5" x 5"

From the light green print, cut:
2 strips, 3½" x 20"; crosscut into 6 squares,
    3½" x 3½"

3 strips, 1¾" x 20"

From the medium aqua print, cut:
2 strips, 1¾" x 20"

From the light aqua print, cut:
1 strip, 3½" x 20"; crosscut into 5 squares, 3½" x 3½"

2 strips, 1¾" x 20"

From the medium purple print, cut:
2 strips, 1¾" x 20"

From the light purple print, cut:
1 strip, 3½" x 20"; crosscut into 4 squares, 3½" x 3½"

2 strips, 1¾" x 20"

From the medium yellow print, cut:
2 strips, 1¾" x 20"

From the light yellow print, cut:
1 strip, 3½" x 20"; crosscut into 3 squares, 3½" x 3½"

2 strips, 1¾" x 20"

From the dark pink print, cut:
1 strip, 3½" x 42"; crosscut into 8 squares, 3½" x 3½"

8 strips, 1½" x 42"

5 strips, 2½" x 42"

From the dark blue print, cut:
2 strips, 3½" x 20"; crosscut into 10 squares,
    3½" x 3½"

From the dark green print, cut:
2 strips, 3½" x 20"; crosscut into 6 squares,
    3½" x 3½"

From the dark aqua print, cut:
1 strip, 3½" x 20"; crosscut into 5 squares, 3½" x 3½"

From the dark purple print, cut:
1 strip, 3½" x 20"; crosscut into 4 squares, 3½" x 3½"

From the dark yellow print, cut:
1 strip, 3½" x 20"; crosscut into 3 squares, 3½" x 3½"

making the blocks

1. Sew each medium pink 1¾" x 42" strip to a light pink 1¾" x 42" strip to make two strip sets. Repeat with the medium and light 1¾" x 20" strips from the blue, green, aqua, purple, and yellow color families to make the number of strip sets indicated. Cut each strip set into the number of 1¾"-wide segments indicated.

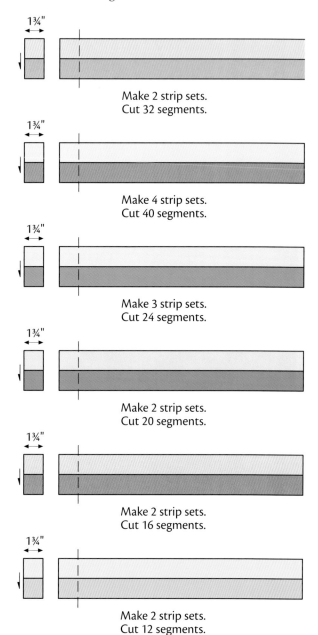

1¾"

Make 2 strip sets.
Cut 32 segments.

1¾"

Make 4 strip sets.
Cut 40 segments.

1¾"

Make 3 strip sets.
Cut 24 segments.

1¾"

Make 2 strip sets.
Cut 20 segments.

1¾"

Make 2 strip sets.
Cut 16 segments.

1¾"

Make 2 strip sets.
Cut 12 segments.

2. Sew two segments from the same color family together to make a four-patch unit. Repeat to make the number indicated for each color family.

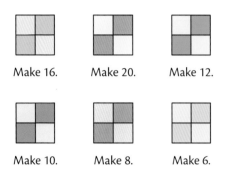

Make 16.   Make 20.   Make 12.

Make 10.   Make 8.   Make 6.

3. Layer each light 3½" square with a dark 3½" square from the same color family, right sides together, with the light square on top. Using a pencil and a rotary-cutting ruler, draw a diagonal line from corner to corner on the wrong side each light square. Stitch ¼" from each side of the marked lines. Cut the squares apart on the marked lines. Each pair will yield two half-square-triangle units.

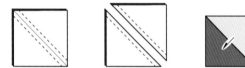

4. Using units from the same color family, arrange two four-patch units and two half-square-triangle units to form a block. Repeat to make a total of 36 blocks.

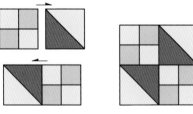

Make 36.

assembling the quilt top

1. Refer to the quilt assembly diagram to arrange the blocks into six rows of six blocks each. Be careful to rotate the blocks as shown to create the pattern. Sew the blocks in each row together, and then sew the rows together.

2. Refer to "Adding Borders" on page 13 to measure the quilt top for borders. Sew the dark pink 1½"-wide inner-border strips to the quilt top. Repeat for the light pink 2½"-wide middle-border strips, and then the dark pink 1½"-wide outer-border strips.

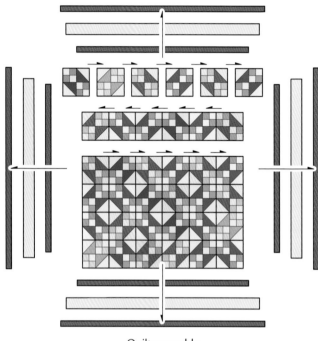

Quilt assembly

finishing the quilt

Refer to "Quilting ABCs," beginning with "Preparing to Quilt" on page 14, for more details on quilting and finishing.

1. Cut the backing fabric so it is approximately 4" to 6" larger than the quilt top.

2. Layer the backing, batting, and quilt top and baste the layers together.

3. Hand or machine quilt as desired. The quilt shown was machine quilted with ovals and loops in the blocks and a ribbon twist in the borders.

4. Trim the batting and backing fabric so the edges are even with the quilt-top edges. Attach a hanging sleeve, if desired, and then bind the quilt. Add a label.

about the AUTHOR

Mary Hickey has been an influential leader in the quilting world for more than 30 years. She continually works to bring new techniques, designs, and ideas to quiltmaking. When she was younger, she taught and lectured all over the world. Now she has turned her energies to creating fresh-looking quilts, clever techniques, and traditional patterns. She lives in the northwestern coastal area of Washington State, where she thoroughly enjoys her family, especially her grandchildren, Audrey, Ava, and Nicholas. Mary loves bird-watching and listening to opera and baseball while stitching on her porch overlooking Liberty Bay.

Mary's primary goal in designing, writing, and teaching is always the same: to design and create projects and write instructions that enable quiltmakers to create beautiful, traditional quilts that look complex, artistic, and stunning but that are easy to make.